Uglier than a
Monkey's Armpit

Uglier than a Monkey's Armpit

Dr Robert Vanderplank

B🌱XTREE

First published in the UK 2007 by Boxtree
an imprint of Pan Macmillan Ltd
Pan Macmillan, 20 New Wharf Road, London N1 9RR
Basingstoke and Oxford
Associated companies throughout the world
www.panmacmillan.com

ISBN 978-0-3304-6448-2

Conceived and produced by
Elwin Street Limited
144 Liverpool Road
London N1 1LA
www.elwinstreet.com

9 8 7 6 5 4 3 2 1

A CIP catalogue record for this book is available from
the British Library.

Additional text by Stephen Dodson
Designed by Jon Wainwright, Alchemedia
Illustrated by Neil Packer

Printed in Singapore

Visit www.panmacmillan.com to read more about all our books and to buy them.
You will also find features, author interviews and news of any author events, and you can
sign up for e-newsletters so that you're always first to hear about our new releases.

Contents

Pronunciation Guide

The words in this book are shown phonetically pronounced by an English speaker, with the stress shown in capital letters. Where some compound words, as in German, have two stresses, the first will be stronger. Some specific vowels and consonants are indicated below.

j- *is the French sound* **j-**, *a soft, slurred jay.*
dj- *is the English sound* **j-** *in jail.*
tch- *is the sound* **ch-** *in chatter.*
ch- *or* **-ch** *is the sound -ch in Scottish loch.*
-onh *is the nasal French sound on.*
-anh *is the nasal French sound in.*
o *is a short* **-o-** *as in hot.*
-oh- *is a long* **-o-** *as in comb.*
-a- *is a short* **-a-** *as in fat.*
-ay- *is the long* **-a-** *as in fake.*
-ah *is a long* **-a-** *as in far.*
-i *is a short* **-i-** *as in dip.*
-ey- *is a long* **-i-** *as in hide.*
-er *is the sound* **-e** *as in the.*
-eh *is the short* **-e-** *as in let*
(used where there is no following consonant.
-u- *is a short* **-u-** *as in put.*

Where translations are marked with single quotation marks, this indicates
a literal translation. Where translations are marked with double quotation marks,
this indicates approximate equivalents.

Introduction

There is something about the well-crafted put-down articulated by a beautiful women against her hapless male companion. Ouch! We wince. Not only do the words wound the recipient, however justly, but the whole of manhood is also bruised by the encounter. For me, insults and curses are the 'dark' side of manners and customs and all the more interesting for that, as they may inform us about what lies beneath the social codes, what verbal games men and women play with each other. Listening out for insults and curses may provide us with as many insights into the local culture as observing local manners and customs. How often have we gained a lasting impression of a village, town or country not by acts of kindness or courtesy but by witnessing or being subjected to rudeness and boorish behaviour?

Increased contact and communication, in my experience, is no guarantee of improved international relations and understanding. Far from it, chatting to the locals may also increase the potential for conflict and misunderstanding, the reinforcing of mutually unappealing stereotypes, the risk of delivering unwitting insults to one's hosts. If you've ever been in a cafe in a far-off place with what appear to be friendly locals, seen the temperature fall for some unknown reason, and had to make a hasty exit owing to some unexplained contravention of local rules, perhaps just a gesture, you'll know what I mean. A mean tip, a deprecating remark which was understood, over-long eye contact with a woman, the wrong finger-sign. "What on Earth did we do or say?" you howl as it is made unequivocally clear that you have caused an insult. Oh, the minefield.

In many cultures, insults are as much a part of social ritual as polite exchanges are. The distinction between personal insults and ritual insults is often subtle and so culture-bound that the unwary stranger should not get involved. I have a foreign friend who would like to be accepted at our local pub but just can't cope with the seemingly insulting banter. Even "How you doing, John, you old wanker?" leaves him speechless. The whole point about such ritual insults and name-calling is that they cannot be taken as having any truth value.

The attitude and intention of the insulter can be crucial to how a potential insult is received. For example, most languages and cultures have the equivalent of the word "poof", and such words can be used jokingly between friends. But for the most part, it can only be used as a joke if no truth-value is intended by the speaker or received by the recipient. Say "poof" to the wrong person in some parts of the world and extreme violence might be the outcome.

In collecting insults and curses, I found many common patterns: insults about appearance and looks, about character and mood, about clumsiness and behaviour, about family, legitimacy and origins, about strength and weakness, about sexual prowess or lack of it, and about husband and wife relationships. Probably the most widespread common theme across languages and cultures is the cuckolded male, though dim-wittedness comes a close second. In some cultures, such as Russian, appearance is a great source of insults, while in others, such as Turkish, physical handicaps still figure strongly. With curses, while there were also common themes such as requests to deities to do awful things to children, both living and unborn, euphemisms to avoid blasphemy, and instructions to go off and perform various sexual acts, there was also a striking contrast between cultures where the curse was alive and taken literally, and cultures where its force had been lost to the extent that those cursing might be ignorant of the literal sense of the words.

It seems that women have different attitudes towards insults than men, on the whole. Men often tend towards swear words, crude obscenities, or name-calling, while women might come out with insights into the insult culture or would think of insults that played more on words than on the shock factor. Some cultures also revealed wide differences between male insults and female insults. In Arabic, for example, I was able to obtain few insults which could be used by both men and women. In Japanese and Chinese, I was told that it was not done for women to insult or curse. In Welsh, in contrast, I can hear the biting (and often back-stabbing) wit of Welsh women. South Africa came out as a rich melting pot of insults, appreciated across its many languages and ethnicities by both sexes.

In the end, insults and curses reveal our common humanity and common traditions. Certainly, the widespread nature of ritualised insults, both geographically and historically, was a revelation. In Italy, for example, there are ritual poetic duels called *contrasti*, in which poets compete to outdo one another in clever and witty insults. Such ritualised insults traditions are found across the world, from the *flytings* of Norse and Anglo-Saxon mythology to the *dozens* of African-American culture and most recently to rap contests.

What I have tried to do is to give the reader insights into the climate and culture of insults in each language and to share the wonderful, shocking, and often hilarious revelations that I experienced in my research.

Robert Vanderplank

Ancient Languages

W e don't take cursing very seriously today; we say "Go to hell!" without any idea of consigning someone to eternal torment, and "Damn it!" is used of things with no soul to damn. In the ancient world, however, people believed in the power of words to do harm, and they availed themselves of it freely. The earliest people whose writings we can read, the Sumerians, described how the goddess Ninhursag cursed the river god Enki: "Until thou art dead, I shall not look upon thee with the eye of life." (Don't worry, she relented and cured him.) The fall of the Akkadian Empire is commemorated in a text called "The Curse of Agade," which features such hair-raising injunctions as "In this city, may heads fill the wells! May no one find his acquaintances there, may brother not recognise brother! May its young woman be cruelly killed in her woman's domain, may its old man cry in distress for his slain wife!" (It seems to have worked; the text ends, "Inana be praised for the destruction of Agade!")

Cursing was part of the official apparatus of the Egyptian state; according to Dr Geraldine Pinch: "The names of foreign enemies and Egyptian traitors were inscribed on clay pots, tablets or figurines of bound prisoners. These objects were then burned, broken or buried in cemeteries in the belief that this would weaken or destroy the enemy." Curses were also used to protect tombs in pyramids, as in this example from the Fifth Dynasty: "As for anyone who shall lay a finger on this pyramid and this temple which belong to me and my *ka*, he will have laid his finger on the Mansion of Horus in the firmament . . . he will be nowhere and his house will be nowhere; he will be one proscribed, one who eats himself." (An earlier inscription says: "Anyone who does anything bad to my tomb, then the crocodile, hippopotamus and lion will eat him." The idea of being eaten seems to have particularly bothered the Egyptians.)

And all over the region – among the Hittites and the Babylonians, and in the Hebrew Bible – treaties and contracts often included curses against anyone who broke them, which became much more elaborate in the first millennium BCE. These Near Eastern traditions were continued by the ancient Greeks, who, besides larding their treaties with curses, developed a tradition of "cursing and binding tablets" called *katadesmoi*, with the victim's name scratched on lead and tossed into a grave or well; the Romans borrowed this along with other aspects of Greek culture, calling the tablets *defixiones*.

Of course, curses and insults have doubtless been uttered as long as people have used language. Already in the earliest known epic, Gilgamesh insults Ishtar so badly that she goes to her parents and complains: "Father, Gilgamesh has insulted me over and over, he's said terrible things about me, despicable deeds and curses!" Her dad tells her to forget it and suggests she must have provoked him. But she talks him into letting her use the Bull of Heaven to get revenge, whereupon Gilgamesh kills the bull and insults her some more. Love has never been easy.

Ancient Greek

G reek literature opens with insults. "Sing, O goddess, the anger of Achilles," begins the *Iliad*. Achilles is angry because Agamemnon first insulted the priest who asked for his daughter back and then not only tells Achilles he's hateful (*ekhthistos*) but announces he's going to take Achilles' own prize, the fair Briseis, away "so that you'll learn how much stronger than you I am". (See below for Achilles' response.) And curses are plentiful as well, in both literature and life; the ancient Greeks were given to having curses inscribed on lead tablets (Plato calls them *katadeseis*) and deposited in tombs for the action of the gods of the underworld.

The richest source of Ancient Greek curses and insults is undoubtedly the plays of Aristophanes. Near the beginning of the *Ecclesiazusae*, for example, Chremes reports to his pal Blepyros what the women (disguised as men) who have taken over the Assembly have been saying about them: "First he said you're a *panourgos* [a scoundrel, ready to 'do anything'] ... then a *kleptes* ['thief'] ... and a *sukophantes* [an informer, literally 'fig-shower']." Later in the play, the insults *kakodaimon* ('possessed by an evil spirit', ill-starred), *anoetos* ('without understanding', fool), and *embrontetos* ('thunderstruck', fool) are tossed around, and a character is told *diarrageies* – 'May you burst!'

oinobares, kunos ommat' ekhon, kradien d'elaphoio
[oi-noh-bah-RESS, kew-nos OHM-mat eh-KHOHN, krah-dee-AYN deh-lah-FOY-oh]
When Achilles gets fed up with Agamemnon's insults, he really lets him have it: 'You drunkard with a dog's eyes and the heart of a deer!' It's all downhill from there.

Arkhilokhon pateis
[ahr-KHI-lo-khon pah-TAYS]
Archilochus, a poet as well as a soldier, was considered by the
Ancients the equal of his contemporary Sappho, but (possibly
because he tended to write about war rather than love) he has
gotten less attention than he deserves in recent centuries. He was
known for his sharp tongue (or pen), and the third-century
Greek biographer Diogenes Laertius quoted "a proverb applied
to those who revile others": 'you are walking in [that is, being a
real] Archilochus'.

katedei pelethon proteros mou
[kaht-EH-day PEH-leh-thon pro-teh-ROHZ moo]
'You'll eat a turd before I will.' A pungent Aristophanic comeback.
Euruproktos is another, meaning 'wide-anused'. A similar epithet is
lakkoproktos, 'cistern-arsed'.

katapugon
[kah-tah-PEW-gohn]
This insult, used by both Aristophanes and Lucian, is literally
'low-rumped' but seems to mean "given to unnatural lust".

pantes men Kilikes kakoi aneres; en de Kilixin heis agathos Kinures, kai Kinures de Kilix
[PAHN-tez MEN ki-li-KES kah-koi AH-neh-ress; EN deh ki-LIK-sin
HAYZ ah-gah-THOHS ki-new-RAYSS, KIGH ki-new-RAYZ deh ki-LIKS]
The *Greek Anthology* is an ancient collection of epigrams, the
verse form in which the Greeks expressed their observations
on life and people, including the less flattering ones; Demodocus
wrote this fine example of ethnic prejudice, which says 'All
Cilicians are bad men; among the Cilicians there is one good
man, Kinyres … and Kinyres is (after all) a Cilician'.

Latin

In Cicero's *Second Philippic* against Mark Antony, after much discussion of the latter's *stupra et flagitia* (debaucheries and outrages) he says, "*sunt quaedam, quae honeste non possum dicere*", 'there are certain things [among your evil acts] which I cannot pronounce with decency', a clever way to imply the very worst behaviour without descending to bad language. But Latin had no shortage of such language.

The basic Latin "bad words" include the nouns *mentula*, 'prick'; *cunnus*, 'cunt'; and *culus*, 'arse(hole)'; and the verbs *futuo*, 'fuck'; *irrumo*, 'have (someone) go down on you'; and *pedico*, 'fuck (someone) in the arse'. (Interestingly, these three activities were all considered proper for an adult male, whereas being penetrated was seen as shameful, a dichotomy quite different from today's heterosexual/homosexual labels.) The noun *merda*, 'shit', and the verbs *caco*, 'shit'; *meio*, 'piss'; and *pedo*, 'fart', seem to have been less offensive though still not a good idea in mixed company.

stultus
[STOOL-toos]
The Romans were as fond of impugning other people's intelligence as we are today, and this word for 'slow-witted, stupid' was quite popular; the Roman playwright Plautus has a character snarl "*Non taces, stultissume?*" 'Won't you shut up, you complete idiot?' Other similar insults are *asine*, 'donkey', and *fatue*, 'fool'.

scelus
[SKAY-loos]
This word for 'wicked act, crime' represents another set of insults that do not involve obscenity; it can be used by itself as an insult

to imply (in the words of the *Oxford Latin Dictionary*) 'one whose very existence is a crime', and the concept embraces such terms as *verbero*, 'one who deserves a flogging', *furcifer* and *cruciarius* (both 'gallows-bird').

mentula tam magna est, tantus tibi, Papyle, nasus ut possis, quotiens arrigis, olfacere
[MEN-too-lah tahm mag-nahst, tan-toos tee-bee, PAH-pee-leh, NAH-soos oot pos-sees, kwoh-tee-ens AHR-ree-gees, ol-FAH-keh-reh]
'Your penis and your nose are so large, Papylus, that you are able to smell (it) whenever you have an erection.' One of the Latin poets most associated with obscene insults is Martial; this is an entire poem by him (6.36).

pedicabo ego vos et irrumabo
[peh-dee-KAH-b-eh-goh VOHS et eer-roo-MAH-boh]
'I'll fuck you (both) in the arse and make you suck my cock.' This is the famous first line of poem 16 by Catullus, the other great master of Latin insult.

Culibonia
[koo-li-BOH-nee-ah]
A jokey name for a woman (presumably a whore), meaning 'nice arse' and modelled on names like Antonia and Pomponia.

flagritriba
[flah-gri-TREE-bah]
'Wearer-out of whips': a servant who keeps misbehaving (one of Plautus's many creations).

nequissimus
[neh-KWIS-sim-oos]
The superlative of *nequam*, 'worthless, depraved', this is a very satisfying adjective to tack on to whatever noun might be appropriate: *Senex nequissime!* 'You old bastard!'

Early English

W hen ancient Germanic warriors were about to fight, they first engaged in a ritual exchange of insults known as "flyting". You can see this, for example, in the Old English poem *Beowulf*, when Beowulf goes to offer King Hrothgar his help against the monster Grendel. The king's jealous thane Unferth ridicules him, saying he had risked his life foolishly in a swimming contest; "I expect worse results if you wait up for Grendel." Beowulf points out that he's killed nine creatures that day and says, "I haven't heard any such stories of *your* fighting ability," adding that Grendel might already have been defeated "*gif þín hige waére sefa swá searogrim swá þú self talast*" ('if your spirit were as fierce as you yourself say'). Similarly, in *The Battle of Maldon* the invading Vikings and the English exchange taunts before the battle.

Following are a selection of words that give further insights into the early cursing culture of the everyday speaker of English. Such a person may be commonly called 'cow-tongued', which according to Thomas Wright's *Dictionary of Obsolete and Provincial English* (1857) found its meaning in the speaker "having a tongue like a cow, smooth one way and rough the other; and hence, one who gives fair or foul language as may suit his purpose".

spatherdab
[SPATH-er-dab]
Middle English has some spectacular words that describe the less than admirable traits of women. A *spatherdab*, used in Leicestershire, according to *Leicestershire Words, Phrases and Proverbs* (1881) is a

"chatterer, gossip, scandal-monger; a woman who goes from house to house dispensing news". On the Isle of Wight, if referred to as a *slackumtrance*, you were being called a "slovenly or dirty woman". And in the English dialect of mid-Yorkshire, *gammerstang* was an insult to avoid. It was directed at a female of idle, loose habits. However, in Lancashire dialect, it referenced simply an awkward, tall, slender person, male or female.

hogs-norton
[HOGZ-nor-tuhn]
This insult finds its roots, according to Thomas Fuller's *History of the Worthies of England* (1662), in the history of a village of the same name. This village, actually called *Hoch-Norton*, was a place "whose inhabitants were so rustical in their behaviour that boorish and clownish people were said [to be] 'born at Hogs-Norton". This insult came to be commonly addressed to any clownish person, unacquainted with the rules of good society. Another similar insult was *gobslotch*, a "greedy, clownish person . . . apt to gobble his food", according to William Holloway's *Dictionary of Provincialisms* (1838).

snorker
[SNOR-k'r]
This word, noted in John Jamieson's *Etymological Dictionary of the Scottish Language* (1808), means "one who smells at objects like a dog". It is derived from *snoke*, meaning "to pry meanly into holes and corners, to poke one's nose where it has no business".

Modern European Languages

T he great cultural influence on Western Europe after the fall of the Roman Empire was, of course, Christianity, and undoubtedly the impressive wording of the ceremony of excommunication ("We declare him excommunicate and anathema; we judge him damned, with the Devil and his angels and all the reprobate, to eternal fire . . .") made an impact on writers like Chaucer, who in his *House of Fame* says of whoever scorns the dream he is about to relate:

> *. . . preye I Iesus god*
> *That (dreme he barfoot, dreme he shod),*
> *That every harm that any man*
> *Hath had, sith that the world began,*
> *Befalle him therof, or he sterve,*
> *And graunte he mote hit ful deserve.*

This was no laughing matter; as he says in the prologue to the *Canterbury Tales*, "*Of cursyng oghte ech gilty man him drede, For curs wol slee, right as assoillyng savith*" ("Every guilty man should fear a curse, for cursing can kill just as absolution saves").

The countries that modernised early – Germany, France, Britain – have let religion slip out of their cursing to a large extent, but others still lean on it; the Scandinavian and Spanish chapters provide good examples, as does this expressive curse from Catalan: *Mecagum Deu, en la creu, en el fuster que la feu i en el fill de puta que va plantar el pi,* or 'I shit on God, on the cross, on the carpenter who made it and on the son of a whore who planted the pine.'

The language experts Damaris Nübling and Marianne Vogel, in a 2004 article in *Germanistische Mitteilungen,* demonstrate that cultures can differ markedly even when using closely related languages, so that Dutch cursing revolves around sex and the female genitalia, German around the buttocks and excrement, and Swedish around God and the devil. They add that the Dutch favour diseases in their imprecations.

In general, Western Europeans do not take profanity very seriously, and they tend to be amused by the anxiety on this topic that often surfaces in America. In 1999, for example, when Michael Bloomberg of Bloomberg Investment Services (a prominent agency for bankers and financiers) decided to ban "inappropriate" language from computers that used his services, the development was widely mocked across the Atlantic. Munich's *Süddeutsche Zeitung* pointed out that a German company using the acronym FAG suddenly had trouble being listed on the New York exchanges because of the homonymy with a forbidden slur. What price freedom of speech?

French

A quaint English euphemism, "Excuse my French", dates back to the late nineteenth century, when it first appeared in *Harper's* in 1895. It neatly captures the stereotype that the French are somehow more permissive, that risqué behaviour and vulgarity are much more acceptable across the Channel. Rather than acting the part that English vulgarity is a foreign language, learn some French curses and insults so that those around you will literally have to excuse your French.

There is no doubt that the French insult and curse very well but, as everywhere, it varies a great deal between generations and from region to region. In Marseille, for example, which has quite a reputation for inventive invective, fourteen-year-old girls hold their own with the boys, and sound that much more shocking.

French insults conjure, for me, the liberated world of adolescent Augusts in La Baule, where I swapped English insults and swear words for French ones with my French exchange friend. I quickly discovered that the French have all the usual lists of forbidden sex, private parts, and unnatural acts with animals, but then go on to embellish them so well. You needn't just tell someone to *va te faire enculer* or "bugger off", you can add *chez les moines*, 'with monks'.

My favourites have always been the explosive expressions of shock or surprise. Who else would exclaim *Putain bordel!* (*putain*, 'prostitute'; *bordel*, 'brothel') and yet use it with as little shock factor as "bloody hell"?

tu me gonfles
[tew muh GONH-fluh]
Used to show surprise and annoyance, this expression makes use of the verb *gonfler*, 'to swell', as in 'you are making me swell'.

Presumably, "you are making me swell with anger and indignation to the point where I'm going to explode". Perhaps more commonly used in the expression *t'es gonflé*, meaning something like "how dare you!" or "what a cheek!" Although not terribly offensive, it is likely that showing such irritation to your elders – surprise, surprise – will not be taken well.

il a un poil dans la main
[eel ah unh pwahl danh la menh]
This enigmatic idiom means 'he has a hair in his hand', a lovely, ridiculous image. The closest English is probably "bone idle" or "bone in his leg", and this tends to be delivered behind the culprit's back, often from their nearest and dearest. "Lazy" doesn't capture the concept in French. You have to think of the *fonctionnaire*, the archetypal French civil servant, who has better things to do than assist you and your needs – and who has "a hair in his hand".

Gesture
When you make this accusation, the correct gesture is to mime pulling a hair from your palm.

One hand should be flat in front of you and the palm should face upwards. Your other hand should hover over the centre of your palm, with your thumb and first finger rubbing together and pulling an imaginary hair from your palm.

il pète plus haut que son cul
[eel pet plew oh kuh sonh kew]
A lovely image, but not a phrase necessarily to say directly to someone's face. It's rude and familiar, and literally means 'he's farting higher than his arse'. Most often heard at work about a boss or colleague who has a very inflated opinion of him- or herself – but you'd be careful about being overheard and wouldn't necessarily use it around the office. It's more the sort of phrase that's dropped in over coffee, most definitely when the person described is not there. Also used to describe a friend who's become big-headed, or a stranger who is snooty and arrogant.

il/elle est bête comme ses pieds
[eel ay bet kom say pyay]
This phrase is very common and is used by all generations to let it be known that someone is very stupid indeed – 'he/she is as stupid as his/her feet'. It is favoured these days by younger people, especially when they are irritated by someone. You can also use the slightly milder version *il/elle est bête* if someone is just being a bit thick.

tu me prends la tête
[tew muh pranh la tet]
Literally 'you are taking my head', this expression is a way of saying that someone is really a pain in the neck. Widely used in France, though perhaps less by older generations, it can mean "stop nagging me" or "you're boring me" and is also used when the person finds something at work or a film plot heavy going.

German

As Stefan Zeidenitz and Ben Barkow write in *The Xenophobe's Guide to the Germans*, "the Germans dearly love to swear and curse, and have any number of explosive epithets with which to do it. Bodily functions are graphically referred to whenever anything goes wrong. *Scheiße*, 'shit', is used so frequently and by so many people that many Germans are not even aware that it is a swear word".

Insulting in German is characterised by a great deal of name-calling. Indeed, the way the language works seems to lend itself to name-calling, as you can form a single word for an epithet which would sound laboured in English. For example, *Sitzpinkler* means someone (a man) who pees sitting down. Somehow, 'sitting-pisser' loses something in translation. We would have to say "I bet you piss sitting down." And what does it mean, anyway? It can mean a weakling in the physical sense, a bit feeble and woman-like, but more often it comes with the accusation of not being able to stand up to a woman.

Of course, there are many German speakers who are not German and who have their own cultures of insults and curses. And indeed, there are many regional insults in Germany itself. Take Bavaria. One of the worst things you can say to someone is that they are *Saupreiß*, Prussian. In German-speaking Switzerland, failure to greet and say goodbye properly can give great offence (as I have observed it can in France). Indeed, ritual greetings are so entrenched in the culture that set phrases exist to describe how people feel about not being greeted properly: *me staat da, wie de Hund am Berg/wie e geklepfte Aff*, 'one is left like a dog on a mountain/like an ape that has been clipped round the ear'. Austria, too, is different. Just as you'll find Scottish versions of English insults, so you'll find Austrian words replace German ones; a good Austrian way to say "scram, beat it!" is *drah di (ham)!* 'turn yourself (home)!', and *Dolm* is the equivalent of the standard German *Dummkopf*, 'dummy'.

Du bist dumm wie Bohnenstroh

[doo bist DOOM vee BOH-nuhn-shtroh]

'You are as stupid as bean straw.' One advantage that German has over English as far as insults go is that even the use of *du*, the informal 'you' instead of the polite and less intimate *Sie* can be a really big insult. Nobody quite knows what bean straw is supposed to be, but it is usually used in the same way as "you're as thick as two planks". 'Straw' crops up again and again as the symbol of stupidity: *strohdoof*, 'as thick as straw'; *der hat nur Stroh im Kopf*, 'he's only got straw in his head'; or the elaborate *der hat seinen Kopf nur, damit er das Stroh nicht in der Hand tragen muss*, 'he has only got a head so that he need not carry the straw in his hand'.

Zu doof zum Scheissen

[tsoo DOHF tsoom SHY-suhn]

If you are regarded as a few bricks short, you will have a rough time in Germany. In Berlin, you might be called *dumm wie Schifferscheisse*, 'as stupid as seaman's shit', an expression which people like because of the alliteration in the double *sch*. You may even be told that you are 'too stupid even to shit': *zu doof zum Scheissen*. *Doof* has more the vernacular sense of 'dumb' or 'thick'.

Schlappschwanz

[SHLAHP-shvahnts]

This insult means 'limp tail'; *Schwanz*, 'tail', is widely used to mean 'penis', so it really means someone who cannot maintain an erection. But these days, not everyone is aware of the origin of that word and it is often used, even to and about women and children, to mean 'weakling'.

Die hat einen Arsch wie ein Brauereigaul

[dee haht eye-nuhn ARSH vee eyne brow-er-EYE-gowl]

'She has an arse like a brewer's dray'. German has a lot of rather crude, physical insults (like English) which centre around *Arsch* or the less vulgar *Hintern*, 'backside'. If you really hate someone, you might come out with *den würde ich nicht mit dem Arsch angucken*, 'I wouldn't look at him with my arse'. And then there's *du Arschloch*, 'you arsehole'; *du Arschkreicher*, 'you arse licker'; and *du kannst mich mal am Arsch lecken*, a very close equivalent of "you can kiss my arse", though even more foul, since *lecken* literally means 'lick'.

Arsch mit Ohren

[ARSH mit OH-ruhn]

This insult is more likely to draw a smile than a punch in the face and is unlikely to offend the younger set, but I suggest avoiding hurling it at your grandmother. Continuing in the vein of the crude physical insult, you may say 'arse with ears' to someone who is being particularly horrible to you. This expression is quite common, to the extent that the epithet was recently applied to a gangster in a German film.

Verdammt!

[fer-DAHMT]

'Damned!' Another variant is *Verflixt!* Religion-inspired cursing is also commonplace in Germany and other German-speaking counties. You'll hear *verflucht*, 'cursed', and *Herrgott*, 'Lord God', everywhere, as well as *Teufel*, 'devil'. Some curses such as *Kruzifix* 'crucifix' are more likely to be heard in the Roman Catholic south.

Warmduscher

[VAHRM-doo-shuhr]

Literally a 'warm-shower-taker'. If you describe someone in this way, you are saying that they are a weakling and unable to rise to any of life's challenges.

Bei dem piept's wohl

[bye DEM peepts VOHL]

This phrase, literally 'He certainly has it squeaking', is addressed, often in the heat of the moment and quite loudly, at another road user to indicate that he or she is completely out of their mind. As in a similar situation in an English-speaking country, it is often accompanied by a less than polite gesture. In German you would *jemandem einen Vogel zeigen*, 'show a bird to someone'.

Gesture

When using this insult, the correct gesture is to tap your forehead with your finger.

In Germany, there is an old folk belief that there are small birds in the heads of people with mental diseases. When you tap your head with your finger, you are questioning someone's mental state.

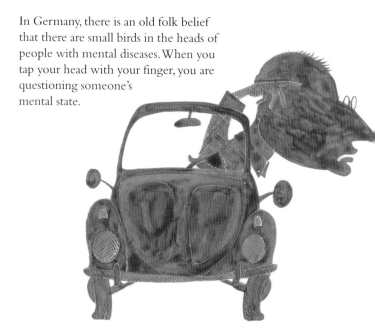

Dutch

T he Dutch have an enviable reputation for tolerance, and much of the Netherlands is notorious as a permissive place where you can buy or do almost anything – within reason, and mostly within the realms of common European taboos regarding sex and drugs. This may explain the extremes of Dutch curses, which, while not bothering with the taboos of personal ancestry and bedroom prowess or lack thereof, tend to go straight to the heart of the matter and suggest that the recipient die in particularly protracted and painful ways.

Many Dutch people, when they want to show just how fed up with someone they are, call a dreadful disease down on their unfortunate victim. Not surprisingly, the less common the disease, such as *de klere*, 'cholera', the less strength behind the insult. In the Netherlands, instead of telling someone to drop dead, you might say *krijg de typhus* to them, or "Go catch typhus!"

The Dutch use genital–oriented words rather than anal words (as in German) to show their anger, and while, on the whole, they are a polite society, if you scratch the surface you soon discover the truth. Indeed, a recent Dutch book exploring cursing in the Netherlands is an impressive 455 pages long.

krijg de kanker achter je hart zodat de dokter er niet bij kan!
[kraykh duh KAHNG-ker akhter yuh HART zo-daht duh DOK-ter air neet bay kahn]
A popular expression in Amsterdam, this phrase goes some way to showing the force of insult you can hurl at someone using a more common disease. While you might tell someone in English "go hang yourself", the same insult rendered in Dutch is much more gruesomely brutal and graphic. Using this idiom in the

Netherlands, you are literally saying, 'Go get cancer behind your heart so the doctor can't reach it!' Probably not the best line to whip out on first meeting someone, but it's handy to listen out for the phrase and, if it's aimed at you, best find out what you've done and make amends.

de matennaaier
[duh MAH-tuh-nah-yer]
Not to be used except in extreme circumstances and with people who know you well. This Dutch term describes someone who is a sneak, who is not well liked by his peers at work. Literally translating as 'mates-fucker', it might be used to insult a person who reports to your boss that you stole a box of pens or that you arrived at work forty-five minutes late two days in a row. Try not to use it in front of a maiden aunt.

de koffer induiken met iemand
[duh KOF-er in-doy-kuh met ee-mahnt]
In the Netherlands you don't have a roll in the hay with someone, you 'jump in a suitcase together' – possibly to elope, but probably suggesting a dirty weekend away. While not the kind of phrase you'd use to initiate a romantic encounter, this is still the sort of schoolyard/sportsground insult that will get a laugh from everyone, except perhaps the person on the receiving end.

kankertyfuslijer!
[KAHNG-ker-ti-feus-layer]

Another way the Dutch use diseases to curse someone can be even more blunt and cutting. It is quite common to declare that someone already has one, or perhaps even two, diseases. Calling someone a *kankerlijer* or 'cancer sufferer' is one thing, but you can pile them on in the Dutch invective and call someone *kankertyfuslijer* or 'cancer and typhus sufferer' instead. An English speaker might have cursed someone by calling "A pox on you!" in the sixteenth or seventeenth century, but it is unlikely that you would receive more than a slightly bemused expression by yelling "Smallpox sufferer" at someone on the streets of London today.

je moeder is een hoer!
[yuh MOO-der iss uhn HOOR]

The ever-popular 'Your mother is a whore!' can be frequently heard chanted at soccer matches, with an opposing player's name added for clarification. And 'your mother is so fat' jokes are popular enough to have web sites especially dedicated to them; a mild one is *Je moeder is zo dik dat ze een eigen postcode heeft*, 'Your mother is so fat she has her own postal code.'

godverdomme
[KHOT-vuhr-dom-muh]

'God damn it!', the strongest curse in Dutch. There is a corruption of this curse, *gadverdamme*, which is less strong. It is used as an exclamation if you were to step in dog excrement or have some other disgusting experience.

Italian

I talians have long used a clever and well-directed insult as a power play. In the sixteenth century, the rich and powerful paid Pietro Aretino to write insulting letters and articles about their political enemies from the relative safety of Venice.

Even today, former Prime Minister Silvio Berlusconi has published a book of insults, *Berlusconi ti odio* ('I hate you, Berlusconi'), full of insults that have been directed at him by his political opponents during his career. Political analyst Franco Pavoncello of Rome's John Cabot University told the BBC, "[Berlusconi] has been the most insulted prime minister since Mussolini." Insults directed at him include extremist, bandit, and even "Premier Pinocchio" (for the lies and for the nose). Berlusconi, for his part, can give as good as he gets and once claimed that Communists eat babies. Nothing much changes in Italian politics.

contrasto
[kon-TRAHS-toh]
A tradition dating back to the Middle Ages, this is a type of sung improvised poetry in which two or three poets take turns offending each other and challenging each other's manhood in verbal duels. For example, Valentina Pagliai quotes a *contrasto* from a festival held near the city of Pistoia:

> *E tu mi piglieresti darl minchione*
> *e così simile a qui ttu compare*
> *ma va fro due pe' comparazione*
> *io son quello che meglio e sá fare*
> *e colle donne ne chiedo ragione*
> *son quello che meglio e gli sa 'ndare*
> *che fra vo du grassi io son secco*
> *ma sihuramente e nun son becco*

You would like to take me for a dickhead
and thus similar to your pal
but between you two, to make a comparison
I am the one who knows how to act the best
and from the women I ask confirmation
I am the one who knows how to go the best
since between you two fat ones, I am skinny
but for sure I am not a cuckold (lit. 'male goat')

campanilismo
[kahm-pah-ni-LIZ-moh]

Regionalism is strong in Italy, and there are a wide range of insults about other towns and regions. The rivalry between cities even has a name, *campanilismo*, literally 'bell towerism', as it was illustrated by each town trying to outdo the other with the size and scope of its local bell tower. A couple of well-known examples of inter-regional insults are *Meglio un morto in casa che un marchigiano alla porta*, 'Better to have a death in the house than someone from the Marche at your door,' and this rhyme:

> *Veneziani, gran signori,*
> *Padovani, gran dottori,*
> *Vicentini, mangia gatti,*
> *Veronesi, tutti matti.*

> Venetians aristocrats,
> Paduans learned,
> Vicentini eat cats,
> Veronesi all mad.

Roma ladrona
[ROH-mah lah-DROH-nah]

Another regional insult, this means 'Rome the big thief' and has been used as a slur on the corruption and inefficiency of the capital. It reflects Northern regionalist and separatist sentiments to the extent that it was used as a political slogan a few years ago by the Northern League political party of Umberto Bossi.

stronzo
[STROHN-tsoh]
Insults have travelled from regions to be common throughout Italy. *Stronzo*, 'piece of shit', was originally Longobard dialect, where *strunz* literally means 'excrement'. This curse then moved to Rome, where it picked up its more figurative meaning, and now *stronzo* is said everywhere.

figlio di papà
[FEEL-yoh dee pah-PAH]
While in other cultures it may be taken as an insult to be called a "mama's boy", in Italy, of course, all boys belong to *mama*. The insult, then, is reversed and you can be called *figlio di papà*, or 'daddy's boy'. It implies that you have got on in life because you have got your father behind you.

avere le mani bucate
[ah-VAY-reh leh MAH-nee boo-KAH-teh]
Italian has some lovely, striking images in its vernacular about behaviour, appearance and stupidity, like this idiom for a spendthrift, 'to have holes in [one's] hands'. Many of the insults about stupidity are mild and friendly, such as *gli manca una rotella*, 'he's missing a wheel'; *cervello di gallina*, 'chicken-brain'; or the slighly more vulgar *che povero coglione, che sei* 'what a poor ball (that is, testicle) you are'.

brutto come la fame
[BROOT-toh koh-meh lah FAH-meh]
The culture and history of Italy are clearly present in this description of someone less than beautiful. Rather than say straight out "You're ugly", the Italian insult 'ugly as hunger' reminds us of relatively recent poverty in the country.

cornuto
[kor-NOO-toh]
Insults about sex or lack of it abound, particularly those linked to being cuckolded. *Cornuto*, literally 'horned', is accompanied by the gesture of raising the index and little fingers while closing the middle two and thumb. Many a referee at a football match has suffered from mass gestures of this type following a disputed decision.

vaffanculo
[vahf-fahn-KOO-loh]
Most famous from an early scene in Shakespeare's *Romeo and Juliet*, this gesture, like another Italian gesture where the fingers are drawn up the cheek and flicked out at the object of your disdain, has a straightforward meaning and could be accompanied by the expletive *vaffanculo*, 'up your arse' (contraction of *Va' a fare in culo*). The meaning of this gesture can be ignored, as it was by the servant of Montague in the play, if it is simply motioned and not accompanied by a verbal insult.

Gesture
Clench your hand in a fist with your thumb extended at the top. Place your thumb between your front teeth and motion biting down on it, in the direction of your target.

puttana

[poot-TAH-nah]

According to lexicographers, *puttana*, 'whore', has the most synonyms in Italian, including *lucciola*, 'firefly', and *zoccola*, 'clog', which has a meaning closer to "slut". Like the French *putain*, with the same meaning, it probably comes from the Latin root found in *putida*, 'stinking', a good illustration of how insulting terms can migrate from one semantic sphere to another.

non si può avere la botte piena e la moglie ubriaca

[non see pwoh ah-VAY-reh lah BOT-teh PYEH-nah eh lah MOHL-yeh oo-bree-AH-kah]

Here is a very nice Italian twist on having your cake and eating it: 'You can't have a full barrel and a drunk wife.'

che casino

[kay kah-SEE-noh]

As elsewhere in Europe, Italians have a sense that there is less propriety these days, driven by TV and other media. My Italian friends give the example of the now common *che casino*, literally 'what a brothel', which would not be acceptable to older generations, to illustrate the change. Now the phrase is just used to describe a mess, either untidiness or a complete cock–up, while *cazzo*, 'dick', is now also ubiquitous as a word expressing irritation or exasperation. As Enzo Biagi wrote in *I come Italiani* in 1972, "In fact, there has been a flooding and flourishing of bottoms, balls, and so on; and 'brothel' stands for noise, confusion, and mess."

sfottere

[SFOHT-teh-reh]

This verb meaning 'to make fun of someone' finds its origins in the south of Italy, where it more particularly attacks male prowess, as it is based on the verb *fottere*, 'fuck'.

Spanish

T he thing to bear in mind about Spanish insults and curses is that many of them sound a lot worse when translated into English than they do to Spanish speakers. A colleague reported how shocked he was when the sister of a friend exclaimed *ay coño*, literally 'oh, cunt', in front of her parents, but this expletive is really considered no stronger than "bloody hell". Like *con* in France, it has lost all physical meaning to the Spanish ear, just as "fuck" and "bugger" have to many English-speaking people. *Puta*, 'whore', on the other hand, retains its force, and combinations with *madre*, 'mother', are so common that in Mexico the latter word tends to be avoided in favour of *mamá*. Another regional variation is that the word *coño* is replaced in the Rio Plate region of Argentina and Uruguay by *concha*, elsewhere in the Spanish-speaking world a harmless word for 'shell' (as well as a nickname for Concepción, a fact which causes much grief for women of that name who move to Buenos Aires).

Likewise, variants of *cago*, 'I shit', are commonplace among all generations and aren't perceived as strongly as they sound in translation. Examples of this include *me cago en la madre que te parió*, 'I shit on the mother who gave birth to you', and *me cago en la leche que te dieron*, 'I shit in the milk you were given.' These two phrases might be directed as an insulting curse to someone who has offended you. Insults between men are often part of banter, and the tendency is for there to be a great deal of friendly insulting among those under forty. Regions play a part too. You'll hear more insults in central Spain than, say, in the Basque country.

eres un aguafiestas
[EH-rehs oon a-gwah-fee-ES-tahs]
Spanish has any number of ways of insulting people's character
and behaviour. If you are a party-pooper, then you are literally
being told, 'You're a wet fiesta'.

vaya al diablo
[BAH-yah ahl dee-AH-bloh]
This phrase is a general curse to 'go to the devil' and a weaker
substitution for *vete al carajo!* or 'go to hell!' It, along with this
gesture, is used widely in all Spanish-speaking countries. This
phallic gesture can mean "up yours" in practically any European
country and is used much in the same way as an English speaker
would give someone the finger.

Gesture
Clench your left fist and jerk
your forearm up as you slap
your left bicep with your
right palm.

una bala perdida

[oo-nah BAH-lah pehr-DEE-dhah]

Another great Spanish insult is reserved to describe a good–for–
nothing, useless type of person, especially someone wasting their
life on drink and drugs. This delightful idiom describes such a
person as 'a lost bullet'.

más liada que una calabaza

[mahs lee-AH-dhah keh oo-nah kah-lah-VAH-sah]

The Spanish come down hard on those who want to make life
difficult for others with a number of fruit–, vegetable– and plant–
related put–downs. People who haven't got a clue what they are
talking about may be dismissed as being 'more tangled up than a
pumpkin'. The Spanish variety of pumpkin has particularly
tangled tendrils. If you wind people up or are antagonistic, you'll
be labelled 'the apple of discord', *la manzana de la discordia*.

eres más malo que la baladre

[eh-rehs mahs Mah-lo keh lah bah-LAH-dreh]

One of my favourite Spanish put–downs is a little more garden–
variety. The oleander bush is very toxic and when it grows wild
(*borde*) it can take over a garden. Suffice to say it is definitely not
something you want in your garden. I think the undercurrents
in *eres más malo que la baladre*, 'you are meaner than oleander',
are now quite clear.

te enrollas más que una persiana

[teh en-ROH-yahs mahs keh oo-nah pair-see-AH-nah]

If you never get to the point and won't stop talking, you'll be told
'you are getting more rolled up than a blind'. This put–down is a
neat play on the word *enrollar*, 'to roll up (a blind)', which is also
used for 'to talk a lot'.

estás en la higuera

[es-TAHS en lah ee-GEH-rah]

The Spanish don't like stupidity and give behaviour perceived as stupid a hard time. This means 'you are in the fig tree'; another expression is *eres más tonto que un higo*, 'you are more stupid than a fig'. Animals join the floral put-down for more pointed insults about stupidity, like *eres un borrico*, 'you are a donkey'. Grapes figure in the lovely *eres más tonto que Abundio que se fue a vendimiar y se llevaba uvas de postre*, 'you are more stupid than Abundio who went to pick grapes and took grapes for dessert'.

eres más tonto que mear de pie

[eh-rehs mahs TON-toh keh meh-AHR deh PYEH]

Getting away from the fruit and vegetables, an insult that women may find particularly useful is this one, 'you are more stupid than peeing standing up', a euphemistic insult if ever I've heard one.

duro de mollera

[DOO-roh deh moh-YEH-rah]

'Having a hard head' used to mean "hard-headed" in the English sense of stubborn or even pragmatic, but these days the Spanish meaning is closer to "block-headed" in the sense of stupidity. Clever people may be compared to *un águila*, 'an eagle', in the sense of being eagle-eyed or perceptive; more negatively, they may be likened to a lynx – a common insult for someone who is a bit of a smart-alec is *eres más lista que un lince*, 'you're smarter than a lynx'. But the ultimate is to be cleverer than hunger, *más listo que el hambre*. Hunger always finds a way to get you no matter where you hide.

eres más fea que los sobacos de un mono

[eh-rehs mahs FEH-ah keh lohs soh-VAH-kohs deh oon MOH-noh]

Insults about appearance tend to be comparative and to be pretty nasty sounding, if often delivered humorously or indirectly about a third person. How would you like to be told, as in the phrase *eres más fea que los sobacos de un mono*, that 'you are uglier than a monkey's armpit'? Or that 'you are uglier than hitting a father', *eres más feo que pegarle a un padre*? Just as it is not nice to hit your own father, so it is not nice to be ugly.

ves menos que un pez por el culo

[behs MEH-nohs keh oon PEHS por el KOO-loh]

Spanish insults get funnier and funnier to our ear when you consider that people who can't quite see the point of something may be told that 'you see less than a fish through his arse', or even *ves*

menos que tres en un burro, 'you see less than three people on a donkey'.

eres más gandul que el suelo

[eh-rehs mahs gahn-DOOL keh el SWEH-loh]

A lazy person may be told 'you're lazier than the floor'; it's a crime, it seems, to lay there and do nothing. An ill-mannered person may be humbled by *eres más bestia que un arado*, 'you're more of a beast than a [peasant's] plough', or *eres más gandul que la zapatilla de un gitano*, 'you're lazier than a gypsy's shoe'.

ojalá te caiga un rayo y te mate

[oh-khah-LAH keh teh KYE-gah oon RAH-yoh ee teh MAH-teh]

And to finish, a really good curse, 'Let's hope you are killed by a lightning bolt'. The word *ojalá*, the 'Let's hope' part of the curse, derives from the Arabic *law sha'a Allah*, 'if God would wish'.

Portuguese

Male culture in Portugal accepts insults as part of the banter between friends, and as part of the café culture, especially after a few drinks. Football fans, too, are known for the ritualised exchanges with supporters of rival teams, such as *e quem não salta e paneleiro*, 'if you don't jump you're gay', or *e quem saltou no cu levou*, 'whoever jumped was buggered', and workers on building sites still feel almost an obligation to shout obscenities such as *fodia-te essas mamas todas*, 'I'll fuck your tits'. In general, male-to-male culture can be pretty crude, so the foul-sounding *cona insonsa*, 'pussy without salt', is not said to insult or hurt but to say that someone is a good chap.

In most of Portugal, women leave the cursing, swearing and insulting to men, but the north, in towns like Porto, Caminho and Braga, has its own customs, and women, together with men, sprinkle slang and obscenities in their language without thinking, especially in the rural parts, where you'll hear *caralho*, 'cock, prick', used in the same thoughtless, reflexive way the English "fuck" is now heard. (It can be used on its own – "Damn!", "Shit!" – or as part of an insult: *Estúpido do caralho!*, 'You fucking idiot!')

We should not forget the wonderfully rich insult and cursing culture of Brazil. Carlos Lacerda, a journalist and politician, once said, "Brazil is the only country in the world where practically every word is a cuss word, even 'mother'". Again, men are more likely to use insults than women, and women are more likely to add the diminutive suffix *-inho* to incorporate an affective tone to their insults. Insults are often used following *seu/sua* (literally 'your', but in these cases to be read as "You . . ."). When hearing an insult, people might respond using *É a sua mãe!* ('It's your mother!'), or, less strongly, using *É a vovozinha!* ('It's your little granny!')

Brazilians can usually find something to insult, whether it's sexual orientation (*veado*, 'deer', or *fresco*, 'fresh', both meaning "gay"), nationality (*galego*, 'Portuguese', *gringo* for anybody who isn't Brazilian), or bad driving skills (*barbeiro*, 'barber', and *roda presa*, 'locked wheel').

---

tua mãe é uma vaca
[too-ah MYNH eh oo-mah VAH-kah]
Quite a few Portuguese insults involve cuckoldry or insults about one's mother. 'Your mother's a cow' really means that your mother cheated on your father, as does *o corno do teu pai*, 'the horns of your father', both often accompanied by this famous two-fingered gesture. The Brazilians will use *cu da mãe*, 'mother's arse', for any undefined location: "*Onde ponho isto?*" "*Põe no cu da mãe*" ("Where do I put this?" "Put it where the sun don't shine").

Gesture
Clench your right fist and extend your thumb and smallest finger. Extend your arm and thrust it forcefully towards your victim.

vai pentear macaco!

[vie pen-tee-AHR muh-KAH-koo]
Cursing is often done through the command *vai*, 'go', followed by
an action: 'Go comb a monkey!'

havias de ser enrabado até à morte

[ah-VEE-ahz dee sehr en-rah-BAH-doo ah-TEH ah MOR-tee]
As everywhere, intonation and intention may change the force
of an insult or curse. On the face of it, 'you should be sodomised
until you die' looks like a very offensive curse, but it can be used
in a friendly way (believe it or not) unless directed at a gay
person, who might find it too literal and take it as an insult. For a
more friendly, jokey curse, try *havia de te nascer um pinheiro no cu*
'may a big pine tree grow out of your arse'.

quem não sabe foder até os colhões estorvam

[kaynh nownh sah-bee foh-DAIR a-TEH oos kol-YOEENHS es-
TOR-vanh]
People who appear naive about sex are told, 'If you don't know
how to fuck, your balls get in the way'.

tu és um borra-botos

[too ess oom bo-rah-BOH-toos]
A clumsy and stupid person is told, 'You shit in your own boots'.
Someone who behaves really stupidly may be told the intense
não vales o ar que respiras, 'you don't deserve the air you breathe',
or that they are *cabeça de alho chocho* – meaning either a 'rotten
garlic head' or a garlic kiss on the lips.

Greek

C rude insulting and cursing are generally considered pretty vulgar and bad manners in Greece, particularly by women, and, in addition, there are two very sensitive topics for insults and curses in Greek which readers would probably do well to steer clear of: other people's mothers and other people's religions. The worst insults you can land on anyone are *gamo ti mana sou*, 'fuck your mother'; *gamo tin Panagia sou*, 'fuck your Madonna/Virgin Mary'; and *gamo to Khristo sou*, 'fuck your Christ'. There is something about the use of *sou*, 'your', which makes these insults particularly strong and offensive. You'll hear Greek taxi drivers use them to other drivers who enrage them, or between men when tensions run high. Sometimes the possessive pronoun *mou*, 'my', is used instead of *sou* in order to signify a sort of inversion of the action towards the user. In that context you will hear people say *gamo ton bela mou*, 'fuck my troubles', or *gamo to kerato mou*, 'fuck my horn', in a kind of soliloquy. This form of self-cursing is meant in both cases as a kind of protest about the troubles or difficulties bestowed upon the person using the invectives. Finally, the use of the Turkish word for 'fuck you', *ai siktir*, is also very common, due to the close proximity with Turkey and the millions of refugees who fled from Anatolia in 1922 and after.

kathisterimene!

[kahth-ee-stair-ee-MEH-neh]

Like most cultures, Greek has some very direct insults for the inept or badly organised; this one, addressed to someone the speaker considers stupid, literally means 'retarded'. *Khameno kormi*, 'lost body', is a common insult for being useless, and the nicely onomatopoeic *kopane*, 'pestle', for a blockhead; an expressive insult along the same lines is *dhen ehis koukoutsi mialo*, 'you don't have (even) a (fruit) pip of a brain'.

kathiki
[kahth-EE-kee]
If someone is being a mean bastard, he can be called a 'pisspot'.

ta ekanes thalassa
[tah EH-kah-nes THAH-lah-sah]
If you say the wrong thing to the wrong person, you might be told 'you've made a sea of things' – as we'd say, "You've really put your foot in it".

then vastoun ta kotsia sou
[dhe(n) vahs-TOON tah KOHTS-yah soo]
If, on the other hand, you don't say the right thing because you're afraid of the consequences, you may hear 'your ankles can't support you' – in other words, you're a coward.

keratas
[keh-rah-TAHS]
What is it about hot Mediterranean countries and their preoccupation with being cuckolded? Watch out if someone calls you *keratas*, 'horned' (in the sense of having antlers) – they are suggesting that your wife is cheating on you. Honour may come into play in insulting. After all, to Greeks, the concept of *filotimo* or *filotimia*, 'love of honour', is what makes a Greek a Greek. It is your *filotimo* that makes you respond to requests, be respected by others, and show courage and individuality. Someone who doesn't have this virtue is *afilotimos*, 'having no sense of honour'.

mamothrefto
[mah-MOH-thref-toh]
This adjective means 'brought up by mum', in other words a mother's boy. A common but quite mild insult to a man.

malaka

[mah-LAH-kahs]

This insult, literally 'wanker', is so frequently used that it has come to mean 'mate' when used between young people, and even women friends can refer to one another as 'wankers'. Try it with older people, and you'll insult them, though, and you have to know your Greeks pretty well before you can safely say *Re malaka!* 'Hey wanker!'

moutza

[MOOD-zah]

Widely used in Greece and parts of Africa, the action roughly means "eat shit". The *moutza* refers to the ancient Byzantine practice of villagers thrusting excrement in the faces of chained criminals paraded around town. In modern Greece, any outward hand motion is deemed extremely offensive.

Gesture

Display your open palm with your fingers spread apart. Your hand is directed to the recipient of the gesture with a jabbing action.

English Language

"**B**ad language" is such a basic part of English that the word *language* all by itself has been used to refer to it. Dickens's Mr Licensed Victualler "never allowed any language", and a character in CC Martindale's 1929 novel, *Risen Sun*, says "I have heard more 'language' in a 'gentleman's' club in ten minutes than in all that evening in the Melbourne Stadium". Furthermore, it was a relatively accepted aspect of English even in Shakespeare's day – not that he actually used the most forbidden words, but he clearly alluded to them ("Do you think I meant country matters?"), and he revelled in vigorous insults. In *King Lear*, when Oswald asks the Earl of Kent, "What dost thou know me for?" the latter replies, "A knave; a rascal; an eater of broken meats; a base, proud, shallow, beggarly, three-suited, hundred-pound, filthy, worsted-stocking knave; a lily-liver'd, action-taking, whoreson, glass-gazing, superserviceable, finical rogue; one-trunk-inheriting slave; one that wouldst be a bawd in way of good service, and art nothing but the composition of a knave, beggar, coward, pander, and the son and heir of a mongrel bitch; one whom I will beat into clamorous whining, if thou deny the least syllable of thy addition." He follows that up with "Draw, you whoreson cullionly barbermonger! Draw!" Clearly both playwright and audience enjoyed a good blackguarding, and there was no sense that public speech had to be decorous.

But not long after that, things changed. First, of course, there were the Puritans, who banned the theatre, but even after the Restoration there was a growing sense that people should *behave*. Tony McEnery, in his recent book *Swearing in English*, says:

"Jeremy Collier . . . , beginning with his 1688 work, *A Short View of the Immorality and Prophaneness of the English Stage*, . . . started a debate that was both to change the language used on stage and act as a precursor to the assault by the [Society for the Reformation of Manners] on the language used by the lower classes on the streets . . . . He deplored the use of bad language on stage and claimed that some of the language used on stage clearly breached laws against the use of such language . . . . Collier encouraged the middle and upper classes to set a good example by not using bad language."

This deadening blanket of "Good Behaviour" spread and thickened until by Victorian times it was impossible to represent everyday speech onstage or in print. George Bernard Shaw hated what he called "Comstockery" (after Anthony Comstock, who in 1873 both created the New York Society for the Suppression of Vice and got the United States Congress to pass a law making illegal the delivery or transportation of "obscene, lewd, or lascivious" material) and began the process of blasting it away by using the phrase "not bloody likely" in Act 3 of *Pygmalion*, which created a huge scandal; it took a long time, but after the unsuccessful prosecution in 1977 of Richard Branson of Virgin Records for the use of the word *bollocks* in the title of the record *Never Mind the Bollocks Here's the Sex Pistols*, official Comstockery was dead and buried. Its effects lingered on, however; it was still some years before the second word was restored in the final sentence of Faulkner's 1939 novel, *The Wild Palms*: "'Women, shit,' the tall convict said." This saga is discussed in an essay by Charles Chappell in Reinhold Aman's *Maledicta*, an invaluable journal for anyone interested in the topic of this book.

English-speakers will continue to swear and insult each other in all the traditional venues, but the advent of the Internet has made it possible for material to be picked up and spread around the world instantaneously, opening up new avenues for the propagation of obscure but euphonious terms like *asshat* and *shitweasel*. The corpus of slang terms may grow so large that in the future, unabridged dictionaries will be possible only online, where there are no printing costs and new words can be added as soon as they become popular.

British English

C ontemporary British English insults are difficult to pin down. One reason for this, I suspect, is that we have seen the breaking down of traditional sources of insults. Who uses *cuckold* these days? Yet in many parts of the world calling someone a cuckold would be a grievous insult and grounds for assault. If we consider the traditional areas of insulting – wounds against pride and vanity, wounds against (family) honour, and wounds against manhood and virility – you can immediately see how much has changed in Britain at least. British men are considered so scruffy and unreliable that they are pretty well immune to insults about their appearance and may even take a perverse pride in their ill-assorted clothing and bad haircuts. Insults about manhood are usually reduced to petty name-calling such as *wanker*, *tosser*, *poof*, *poofter* and *pansy*. You don't hear *eunuch* much these days, certainly not in any literal sense. Public challenges to a man's honour and to that of his family tend to be confined to subcultures, such as ethnic cultures which have brought different values and codes of honour with them. For the mainstream, honour and respect have been replaced by the need to be affirmed and liked by one's peers and neighbours. Slurs on characters don't produce duels any longer, and only the rich can afford actions for slander, though "dissing" ('disrespecting', in young black usage) the wrong person in the wrong place may bring swift and violent retribution.

All this said, there are some insults in English which show creativity and which also indicate priorities if not highlight cultural characteristics.

non sunt in coeli, quia gxddbov xxkxzt pg ifmk

This strange-looking line from a poem composed sometime before 1500, besides being an insult aimed at the Carmelite friars of Cambridge, is notable for containing the first known appearance of the venerable word "fuck" – even if disguised! The first part is in Latin, and means 'they are not in heaven, because'; the last four words are in a simple substitution cipher (one letter off) and read *fvccant vvivys of heli* 'they fuck [in fake-Latin] wives of Ely'. The first printed use comes a few years later, around 1503, from the pen of the Scots poet William Dunbar, a master of abuse who in the course of a verse-quarrel with another poet called him *wan fukkit funling*, a 'fucked foundling' (not to mention *cuntbitten crawdon*, a *crawdon* being a coward). The word *fuck* was not decriminalised in Britain until 1960, only appearing in dictionaries after 1965.

bastard

Literally 'child of unmarried parents', this is a real all-purpose insult in English along with *bugger* (literally 'sodomite'). Neither of these tends to be used as slurs on either the family honour or on the manhood of the recipients these days. *Bastard* and *bugger* have switched to being fairly mild insults about how disagreeable, cruel or unpleasant a person is: "He's a right bastard to deal with" or, often with humour and irony, "You bastard, how could you do that to me?" But both *bastard* and *bugger* have gone further to become coat-hanger words for insults or just comment, as in "you mean, conniving, two-faced, despicable bugger", or, throwing in a curse for good measure, "you lucky bastard".

a few bricks short of a full load

This is the basic form of an insult meaning 'stupid, dim-witted, not quite right in the head, not sensible' that has many variants beginning "A few . . . short of . . .": a few pints short of a gallon, a few sandwiches short of a picnic. In similar vein are "not the brightest star in the sky" and "not the brightest crayon in the box". A cruel one which I once got into trouble for when I used

it with students: "Did you leave your brains at the gate?"
Offended, insulted, high dudgeon! An old expression, less heard
these days, for a clumsy and dim person, often used affectionately,
is *lummox*.

couldn't organise a piss-up in a brewery

There are many variants on this theme of general uselessness, such
as "couldn't organise an orgy in a brothel". A similar base form of
insult begins "about as much use as . . ." and produces many
variants on this theme, such as "about as much use as a fart in a
colander" and "about as much use as a fart in a wind tunnel".

mutton dressed as lamb

This phrase describes an older woman trying too hard to look
younger through her appearance. Another basic one that has
some variants is "you look like you've been pulled/dragged
through a hedge backwards" for someone whose hair needs
brushing or whose general appearance is unkempt. Often, insults
about appearance have a moral edge. For example, "all fur coat
and no knickers" has long been one of my favourites to describe
a person who is all appearance and no substance, carrying with it
the imperative to look after the basics before turning to luxuries.
Best said in an Aberdonian or Morningside (Edinburgh) accent,
with just a hint of prim.

pillock

'Idiot'. You could almost decide, having read this dictionary, that
any unknown British word is most likely to mean 'idiot', and you
could almost be right. We have so many because different ones
sound better in different sentences. On the subject of the word in
hand, it may be a contraction of the sixteenth-century word
pillicock, 'penis'. It's funny, even if it's not true . . .

American English

T he United States was not, by and large, settled by the polite upper crust; it was settled by people who worked hard, drank a lot (three and a half gallons of alcohol per year per person) and used a lot of bad language. But they didn't rest content with a few words endlessly repeated – they gloried in the inventive magniloquence of their exuberant bad-mouthing. As HL Mencken said in *The American Language* (1921), "The American, from the beginning, has been the most ardent of recorded rhetoricians. His politics bristles with pungent epithets; his whole history has been bedizened with tall talk; his fundamental institutions rest as much upon brilliant phrases as upon logical ideas". The master, in this as in so much else, was Mark Twain; we can no longer hear him turn the air blue, but we can take the word of Albert Bigelow Paine's *Mark Twain, a Biography* (1917):

A word here about Mark Twain's profanity. Born with a matchless gift of phrase, the printing-office, the river, and the mines had developed it in a rare perfection. To hear him denounce a thing was to give one the fierce, searching delight of galvanic waves. Every characterization seemed the most perfect fit possible until he applied the next. And somehow his profanity was seldom an offense. It was not mere idle swearing; it seemed always genuine and serious. His selection of epithet was always dignified and stately, from whatever source – and it might be from the Bible or the gutter.

That spirit has continued, if perhaps diminished (like the liquor consumption); Americans still prefer a roundhouse punch delivered with panache to a clever rejoinder à la Oscar Wilde. A century after Twain comes this wonderful attack from Ralph Ellison's *Invisible Man*: "Bledsoe, you're a shameless chitterling eater! I accuse you of relishing hog bowels! Ha! And not only do you eat them, you sneak and eat them in private when you think you're unobserved! You're a sneaking chitterling lover!"

Here are some more pungent put-downs from American soil.

---

mooning

This is considered a rude and insulting act, and the gesture expresses protest, scorn, disrespect or provocation. It is often associated with the pranks and hijinks of college undergrads, and entered student slang, meaning "to flash the buttocks", in 1968. Before this, *mooning* was slang for "romantically pining" after someone or "wandering idly".

Interestingly, in 2006, a court in Maryland determined that mooning is a form of expression protected by the United States constitutional right of freedom of speech.

Gesture

Clothing is removed to display one's bare buttocks, directing them at the recipient of the gesture.

pissant

This satisfying word came over from England as a mere name for an ant, but Americans made it a contemptuous epithet for an "insignificant, contemptible, or irritating person". From HL Davis's 1935 novel, *Honey in the Rock*, about pioneer Oregon: "Anybody who called owning horses disorderly conduct was a liar and a pissant."

come on, long-eared motherfucker, it's gonna be you and me

A line (addressed by a lion to an elephant) from the traditional African–American poem "The Signifying Monkey", whose titular protagonist descends, according to the scholar Henry Louis Gates, Jr, from the Yoruba trickster god Esu.

the jury has found you guilty of being a red-neck, white-bread, chicken-shit motherfucker

An immortal line from Dr Dre's rap song "Fuck Tha Police".

silk stockings

This term, at the end of the eighteenth century simply a reference to the well-to-do in the brand-new United States, a century later had insulting overtones. It had plenty of company: the upper crust (a term used from the 1830s on) were also called *fancy-pants*, *high-hats*, *Mr Moneybags* (or *Gotrocks*), *snoots*, *stuffed shirts*, and (in New York City, where their natural habitat was Fifth Avenue) *Avenoodles* (a term used by Walt Whitman in 1856 and still in use in 1900).

Hell's Kitchen

This vivid term for what in the late 1850s was a mixed black and Irish slum on the west side of Manhattan is still in use, though real estate values in the neighbourhood have risen considerably (and realtors are trying to persuade people not to call it that). Other unsavoury neighbourhood names (no longer in use) listed in Irving Lewis Allen's comprehensive *The City in Slang: New York Life and Popular Speech* are Misery Row, Bandits' Roost, and Mixed-Ale Flats.

Other Englishes

Wherever English has spread, it has developed new forms of invective. Some of the most distinctive dialects are those of the Caribbean, where *rass* (pronounced "rahs", with the *a* of *father*) is perhaps the worst of all swear words – Richard Allsop's *Dictionary of Caribbean English Usage* calls it "an obscene expression of anger or astonishment" and says "its use aloud in public is punishable by law in most territories". (It probably derives from the Dutch *razen*, 'to rage, rave', but has been influenced by a homophonous word meaning 'arse'.)

Whether they are modern United Kingdom dialects or the curse words of the Commonwealth, each gives a flavour of the local region.

like a fart in a trance
(Glaswegian/Scottish English)
This Glaswegian expression is used of a dreamy person who always seems at a loss what to do: "Away oot fur gooness sake instead a hingin aboot the house lik a fart in a trance!" Someone with an inflated opinion of himself will be cut down to size with "He thinks he's big but a wee coat fits him."

shit-disturber
(Canadian English)
This appears to be one of the few genuinely Canadian insults; it refers to anyone who causes more of a ruckus than seems appropriate.

hoser
(Canadian English)

This word, meaning 'idiot' or 'boor', is what first comes to mind when you ask most people to name a Canadian insult; it was apparently used in some quarters before it was popularized by the Bob and Doug McKenzie characters from SCTV, but since then it has hardly been possible to use it except ironically.

dag
(Australian English)

A light-hearted, rather endearing insult, but one all the same, it is directed at someone who is a bit stupid and/or goofy. Literally describing the bits of manure that stick to the long wool around a sheep's bottom, it's worth ignoring its etymology.

drongo
(Australian English)

A *drongo* describes a stupid, inept, awkward or embarrassing person. Alternatively you could use *galah*, *galoot* or *dimwit*.

munter
(New Zealand English)

This insult describes someone who is slightly aggressive, but a little dim. *Boho* is also a popular insult, a bit dismissive and slightly negative, a little like the Australian English *feral*, describing someone who is along for a free ride. *Boho* has a hippy edge.

eye-power
(Singaporean English)

This quaint insult refers to someone who sits back and watches others do the work. The X-Men comic book character Cyclops is sometimes used to describe someone who uses *eye-power* all the time. "*Whoa, we do all the work, you sit there do nothing, your eye-power very good hor?*"

Celtic Languages

What characterises these cultures and languages is the joy of playing with language and displaying linguistic virtuosity in delivering insults. The more biting the insult, the less obscene it is likely to be, and the more striking the image. Obscenity tends to be humorous and is often found in specific contexts such as rugby clubs and rugby songs. When I was growing up in 1950s Wales, swearing or a vulgar insult could mean being sent to bed early with no supper. I only found out recently that my family was fairly typical in this regard. In *William Jones*, a novel by T Rowland Hughes set in Wales during the Depression, the hero, at the end of his tether with his wife (who won't cook his supper), finally cracks and lets forth with *Cadw dy blydi chips*, 'Keep your bloody chips'. I would certainly have gone to bed hungry for this. As for Ireland, as David Ross wrote in *Never Throw Stones at Your Mother: Irish Insults and Curses* (2001), few nations could assemble such an extensive lexicon of lethal weapons as the Irish, or make a mother cry by telling her that she's no more use than a chocolate teapot.

Welsh is full of wise put-downs, such as *dysgu pader i berson*, 'teaching a parson a prayer', and *yr oen yn dysgu i'r ddafad bori*, 'the lamb teaching the ewe how to graze', the equivalent of teaching grandmother how to suck eggs. My favourite Welsh put-down is probably *Codi pais ar ôl piso*, 'to raise one's petticoat after peeing'. It's just such a wonderful image of an action taken too late, but it's also used in other situations such as becoming pregnant unintentionally.

Prior to Wales's nonconformist (and thereby puritan) conversion, Wales had considerably more vulgar poetry and coarse language, much of which has been destroyed or forgotten by the following generations. An example of this is Rhys Jones of Blaenau, who, along with being a regular churchgoer in the late eighteenth century, was one of the organisers of a monthly "Lunatic" society. On the Thursday before the full moon they would gather to drink till they dropped and recite poetry of their sexual conquests, satirising the Methodists and generally being outrageous. Not many of his poems have survived, but most that have appear in a book published by his grandson that censors the worst curse words and comes with a foreword apologising for his grandfather's crassness.

mefl ar dy farf!
[MEH-v'l ar duh VAHRV] (Welsh)
'Shame on your manhood!' A good example of a vigorous Old Welsh curse from the *Mabinogion*, a collection of prose stories from Medieval Welsh manuscripts.

angel pen ffordd, diawl pen pentan
[AHN-gel pen FORDH, DEE-aool pen PEN-tahn] (Welsh)
Someone who is kind in public but cruel to his or her family is 'the angel of the street, the devil of the home'.

hen sguthan
[hen SKEW-hahn] (Welsh)
If you really want to be nasty about someone, call them 'an old wood pigeon' – just don't say it in front of children.

fel piso dryw yn y môr

[vel PEE-soh DREW uhn uh MOHR] (Welsh)

Something ridiculously small is likely to be derided as 'like a wren's piss in the sea'.

gleadhrach na tobhta

[GLEOO-rikh nuh TOH-tuh] (Scots Gaelic)

This Scots Gaelic term from Barra in the Western Isles means 'prattling of the *tobhta*'. The houses in the Western Isles were all stone-built with very thick dry-stone walls, and the broad outer wall-head (which eventually grassed over) was called the *tobhta*. The *tobhta* was an ideal place to lie and soak up the sun (especially for dogs), and given that the houses were often built into the sides of hills, you would sometimes find sheep (and occasionally cattle) grazing on them. At any rate, this expression refers to women who would stand on the *tobhta* and call their husbands to dinner or harangue their neighbours in a quarrel.

thalla is tarraing!

[HAH-luh iss TAH-rin] (Scots Gaelic)

This expression, literally 'away and pull', is the equivalent of "bugger off"; a variant is *thall 's cagainn bruis*!, 'away and chew a brush!'

taigh na galla (ort)!

[tie nuh GAH-luh (ort)] (Scots Gaelic)

This means 'house of the bitch (on you)' and is the equivalent of "damn you", but can be stretched to a more forceful "fuck off".

gun itheadh an cat thu agus gun itheadh an diabhal an cat!

[guhn IKH-uh uhn kaht hoo ah-guhs guhn IKH-uh an JAH-vuhl uhn kaht] (Scots Gaelic)

In the Western Isles they say, 'May the cat eat you and may the Devil eat the cat!'

mìle marbhphaisg ort!

[MEE-luh MAH-roo-feshk ort] (Scots Gaelic)

This poetic Gaelic curse means 'a thousand death shrouds on you'.

blether

[BLE-dher] (Scots English)

You'll be described, with an overtone of endearment, as a *blether* if you chatter incessantly.

besom

[BIZ'm or BEE-z'm] (Scots English)

A woman of low moral standing or a female upstart is a little less politely described as a *besom*.

imeacht gan teacht ort!

[IM-yuhkht guhn tyakht ort] (Irish Gaelic)

This Irish curse means 'May you leave without returning!'; a comparable expression is *titim gan éirí ort*, 'May you fall without rising'.

mórán cainte ar bheagán cúise

[MOH-rawn KINE-chuh ehr BYOH-gawn KOO-shuh] (Irish Gaelic)

This is how you would be described in Ireland if you were the village gossip. Literally 'much talk on a little cause', it describes the idle chatter that is indulged in all too readily.

cac ar oineach

[KAHK ehr IN-yuhkh] (Irish Gaelic)

Literally 'shit on honour', colloquially this insult means "scumbag" or "scoundrel", the local scoundrel being the one without honour.

Eastern European Languages

B ob Cohen, musician and scholar of languages and cultures, says that Eastern Europe can be divided into two main spheres of swearing, that of Central Europe and that of the Balkans. In the Balkans, the use of "targeted blasphemy" is common, in which one may say "Fuck your Christ" or "Fuck your Virgin Mary", the "your" implying that it is only a perverted version of the true Christ or Mary that is under discussion, thus preserving the speaker from actual blasphemy. As one moves into Serbia and Macedonia, the occurrence of swearing using the verb "to fuck" becomes so widespread that "fuck" almost loses its obscene aspect and has to be expanded on in order to offend.

The most entertaining introduction to the topic of Balkan cursing is an account by journalist Bernard Nežmah of an international conference on swear words held in honour of a philologist who had predicted in 1973 that "the development of socialism would lead to a society free of conflict, where there would be no reason for swearing"; Nežmah says "participants brought fresh reports showing quite the opposite." He quotes Dr Nedeljko Bogdanović on "the difference between curses and swearing: the first merely degrades, while the second is malicious. So someone curses you with a blow to your favourite tree in your garden, throwing out: 'May it never grow plums!' while someone swears at you to belittle your greatest pride: 'Fuck you *and* your plums!'" He adds a telling observation: "Even though Yugoslavia was a land often characterised by inter-ethnic tension, swear words were one thing the national groups freely borrowed from one another."

An Ottoman traveller among the Albanians several centuries ago warned others what they might expect in the way of Albanian greetings and salutations. His list included "Eat shit!", "I'll fuck your wife" and "I'll fart in your nose." They still say similar things, as well as *u mbytsh në gjakun tënd*, 'May you drown in your own blood', and *të vraftë Zoti*, 'May God kill you'.

Hungarian has the dubious achievement of having been voted the language in which obscenity occurs most frequently. Swearing is so essential in Hungarian that there is a joke about God coming to Transylvania seeking a chosen people who would accept his commandments: the Hungarian refuses the offer because the commandment against swearing would render him speechless (the Romanian is offended by "thou shalt not steal", the Turk by "thou shalt not kill"). With such a central role in colloquial speech, most swear words have a euphemism attached. When faced with a quandary, one can exclaim "*baassszzz-us kulcs!*" – which starts off sounding like it's going to be *bassz*, 'fuck', but ends up as *basszus kulcs*, the harmless phrase for 'bass clef'.

Romanian cursing seems to have fixated on oral sex along the "suck my dick" line, which is curiously absent in Hungarian swearing. And Romanian and Hungarian Romani ("Gypsy") discourse includes such pleasantries as *mo xav tyo kul*, 'I eat your asshole', which can be said when meeting a mother pushing a baby carriage down the street, meaning "Aww, how cute, I could eat him right up". A Roma woman, when angry at the slightest thing, will say *Xas mo mindz!*, or 'Eat my cunt!' In multi-ethnic situations, however, Roma will usually use milder language than others, perhaps out of fear that harder words will lead to violence.

Czech
& Slovak

C zechs have thicker skins than many peoples, so they tend not to be insulted by put-downs, as these are usually meant more in irony than sarcasm. Most insults, even if metaphorical in their way, bear being taken at face value. As František Čermák, Professor of Czech Language at Charles University, Prague, and others have said of countless Czech idioms and phraseological units, insults are firmly rooted in the fairly recent rustic background of the majority of the nation, where urbanisation came fairly late. The same is true of Slovak, which still uses barnyard animals for its insults: a person with poor table manners or personal hygiene is a *nevychované prasa*, 'hog with no manners'; someone with low intelligence, basically harmless and possibly young, is *hlúpe tel'a*, 'a stupid calf'; and *sviňa*, 'pig', is to this day a staple of Slovak political discourse.

komu není zhůry dáno, v apatyce nekoupí
[koh-moo neh-nee z'hoo-ree dah-noh, VAH-pah-tee-tseh NEH-koh-pee] (Czech)
'Who hasn't been granted [talent] from on high, can't get anything for it at the chemist's.' This rebuke is used against someone attempting something beyond his capacity or who is generally a bit dim. Indeed, dimness and gormlessness provide a rich vein of insults in Czech. Someone who is notoriously dim may have said of (not to) him: *Má IQ šustící trávy*, 'He has the IQ of rustling grass.'

koukáš jako tele na nový vrata

[koh-kahsh yah-koh teh-leh nah noh-vee vrah-tah] (Czech)

'You are staring [at it] like a calf at a new gate.' There are many expressions for someone who is looking gormless or staring helplessly at something, such as *Kouká jako husa do flašky*, 'He is staring like a goose into a bottle', or for looking surprised or confused: *Vypadáš, jako když ti uletěly včely*, 'You look as if your bees have flown' and the delightful *Koukáš jako andělíček, když mu uplavalo mejdlo*, 'You look like a cherub who's lost his soap in the bath.'

vypadá to (ten kabát), jako když to kráve ž huby vytáhne

[VEE-pah-dah to (ten kah-baht) yah-koh g'deesh toh krah-veh z'hoo-bee VEE-tahh-neh] (Czech)

'It (that coat) looks as if it's been pulled out of a cow's mouth' – rather like British English's "looks as if it has been pulled through a hedge backwards". Compare the elaborate expressions for the woman who (mistakenly) thinks she looks good: *Vypadáš jako Mona Lisa po vejprasku*, 'You look like Mona Lisa after a spanking' or *Vypadáš jako strašák do zelí*, 'You look like a scarecrow for putting in a cabbage field,'

jména hloupých na všech sloupích, jména volů na každém kolu

[y'meh-nah h'loh-pikh nahf-shekh sloh-pikh, y'meh-nah voh-loo na kazh-dem koh-loo] (Czech)

'The names of fools on every pillar, the names of asses on every post.' This is a nice example of a put-down for the show-off who has faith in his many attributes and consequent renown, and also a good example of how rhyme is used in insult. Equivalent to the ironic "One day you'll go far" with its optional pendant "... and the further the better" is *Jednou z tebe bude něco velkého, jestli tě něco malého nesežere*, 'One day something big will come of you, unless something little gobbles you up.'

nasrat' do rúk a nepustit' k vode!

[NUH-srat doh ROOK UH NYEH-poos-teet GVOH-deh] (Slovak)

Much like their Czech neighbours, the Slovaks use many terms associated with excretion; this expression means 'May someone shit in his hands and not let him get to the water!' Words like *rit'*, 'ass'; *hovno*, 'shit'; and the many derivations of the verbs *srat'*, 'to shit', and *št'at'*, 'to piss', enjoy as much currency as their Czech cognates. The adjective *zasraný*, 'covered in shit', equivalent to "goddamn", is a very popular multipurpose expletive. And the adjective *vyčuraný* (or *vyšt'aný*), 'pissed out', describes a sleazy character, someone who will always survive no matter what it takes. It and its derived noun *vyčuranec* have been widely used to refer to people who quickly adapt to regime changes and seem to prosper under democracy as well as they did back in Communist times.

keby blbost' kvitla . . .

[KEH-bee B'L-bost KVEET-luh] (Slovak)

Someone not too bright may be told 'If stupidity flowered . . .' (the implication being "... you'd be blooming!") Slovakia being mountainous, it is no surprise that many common insults have to do with plants and wood; people who are inflexible and slow on the uptake can be called *drúk*, 'snag'; *poleno*, 'log'; or simply *drevo*, 'wood'.

Hungarian

H ungarians are a cultured and well-educated people who prefer harmony. They are not afraid of confrontations, though, and the language and culture are much more direct than English. Be warned. Their identity is very family focused and relationships are important (*Madarat tolláról, embert barátjáról*, 'You recognise the bird by its feathers', you know who a person is by the friends he keeps). They are often opinionated, though, and as the saying goes, where there are two Hungarians, there are three opinions. Insults (of which there are very many) tend to be indirect and are sometimes based on proverbs and wise sayings. They also tend to be reserved for those whom you know, since social and personal respect are so important.

It is generally accepted that Budapest residents curse more than most rural Hungarians, and in the Hungarian-speaking areas of Transylvania cursing is still considered bad form, so much so that Transylvanian Magyars watching Hungarian television broadcasts are often shocked at the language commonly used. Prime Minister Ferenc Gyurcsany caused quite a ruckus with a speech to his party in which he said, "Hungary is fucked, we fucked it up (*elkurtunk*)," using a particularly vulgar term for "fucked" based on the word for 'whore', *kurva*, instead of *elbassztunk* (using the common verb for fucking, *baszni*).

agyilag zokni
[AW-jee-log ZOK-nee]
This expression, 'mental sock', is often used sarcastically in addition to being a reasonably friendly insult. People will even describe themselves in this way. Hungarian has many expressions for denigrating people's mental capacity, and no one seems to quite know where this nice one came from. A real put-down for

someone who keeps making mistakes would be *te fasz* or *te faszfej*, roughly equivalent to 'you dick' or 'you dickhead'.

anyázás
[ON-yah-zahsh]
Hungarians are famous wielders of obscenity, and many of their favourite curses involve the mother (*anya*), so much so that there is a term for such curses, *anyázás*. The widespread Eastern European fixation with climbing back into the place whence you emerged provides *Menj az anyád picsába*, 'Go into your mother's cunt', a strong way of saying "get out of here!" And *anyázás* can be combined with the equally popular *kurva*, 'whore, bitch', in *A kurva anyádat*, 'Your mother is a whore.' *Kurva* is so common that it can become simply an amplifier: *kurva jó*, 'fucking good', or *kurvára éheztem*, 'I was fucking hungry', are simply vulgar, not shocking.

az Isten faszát
[oz ISH-ten FAW-saht]
Blasphemous curses like 'the Lord's penis' are still alive and well in Hungary, many dating from the times when Hungary was threatened from the East. This particular expression is in widespread use but is considered to be one of the most vulgar expressions, so use it only when you are really angry. The same warning goes for *Az Isten bassza meg*, '(May) God fuck it!' A mild curse word is *fene* (equivalent to "damn(ed)"), used in expressions such as *fene egye meg* (more or less "damn it!") and *a fenébe* (equivalent to "go to hell!"), probably the most common curse in Hungarian.

lófasz a seggedbe!
[LOH-foss aw SHEG-ged-beh]
This extremely vulgar expression, 'a horse's cock up your ass!', is generally considered the Great Hungarian Curse. Its origins may date back hundreds of years to the time of Turkish occupation, when torturing and execution often involved impaling.

Polish

I n Polish, as in other languages, names for animals and for social groups may be used metaphorically to refer to a person's lack of intelligence or skills, their clumsiness in behaviour, or their perceived deviant character. A good example of this is *parszywa owco*, 'you scabby sheep', meaning what we call "black sheep" in English. Other potential candidates are *krowa*, 'cow', and *świnia*, 'swine'. Of course, there are innumerable nouns that directly denote people and their shortcomings, such as *oferma*, 'muff'; *niezdara*, 'duffer' or 'loser'; *niedołęga*, 'oaf'.

Polish is very strong on curses, though younger people tend to find them old-fashioned or bookish these days. A number of quite frequent ones have to do with God and the devil. A classic version is *Niech cię diabli wyrwą!*, 'May the devils carry you away!' There are also *Żeby cię czort porwał!* 'That the devil carry you away' (*czort* is a Russianism); *Idź do licha!*, 'Go to the devil!'; and *Niech cię piorun trzaśnie!*, 'May a thunderbolt hit you.'

A second group of curses relates to disease or some sort of physical incapacitation, such as *Żeby cię jasna cholera (wzięła)!*, 'That the bright cholera (take) you!' Other examples include *Szlag by cię trafił!*, 'A stroke should hit you.'

rany Boskie
[rah-nee BOHS-kyeh]
'God's wounds' is a very common curse. There are several euphemisms for *rany Boskie*, such as *rany Julek* and *rany kota* ('wounds of Julek' and ' . . . of a cat').

kurwa
[KOOR-vah]
The word 'whore' may be used as a curse as well as an insult. Younger people, especially from a non–middle-class background,

may use *kurwa* in virtually every utterance, to stress its content and their positive or negative attitude towards it (just as Russians use *blyad*, which means 'whore'). Middle–class speakers, if not in a state of particular excitement, normally use a euphemistic form such as *kurczę* or *kurde*. In context, both expressions may turn into curses in the proper sense of the word, for example, *Po co, kurwa, to powiedziałeś?*, 'Why did you say that, whore?' The word also appears in compound insults which are then extremely offensive, such as *Kurwa twoja mać!*, 'Your mother is a whore!'

idź do dupy!
[IDZH doh DOO-pih]
'Go to the arse!', meaning "Leave me in peace!" Unavoidably, another group of curses is centred around the digestive system. There are very difficult and ever–changing pragmatic rules at work that govern usage. Curses implying *dupa*, 'arse', are perhaps not always among the most stigmatised: *Nie możesz tego pojąć, dupo wołowa!*, 'You can't understand that, you arse of an ox', meaning "compounded idiot".

gówno z ciebie, nie poeta!
[GOOV-noh s'cheh-byeh, NYEH poh-EH-tah]
Gówno means 'shit': 'You're shit, not a poet.' And *Ty gnoju!*, 'Dung!', is even worse. *Chuj ci w dupę!*, 'A prick in your arse', is also a sign of extreme disregard.

nie pieprz!
[nyeh pyehpsh]
'Don't talk nonsense'; *Pierdol się, stary!*, 'Piss off, mate.' There are two verbs which have moved into the very centre of Polish slang, *pieprzyć*, 'to pepper', and *pierdolić* (absent in the standard language). They may appear with different prefixes and have a wide variety of meanings, besides 'fuck' also 'beat up', 'talk nonsense', 'not give a toss' and others.

zjebany jesteś!
[zyeh-BAH-nih YES-tesh]
This insult, 'You're fucked', involves the very strong vulgarism *jebać*, 'fuck', which is also found in the equally offensive *Masz najebany we łbie*, 'You are fucked up in your head.' In the same vein, we find *A niech was chuj!*, 'May the prick [fuck] you,' and *Ty chuju!*, 'You prick!'

niech cię nie znam!
[nyekh chenh nyeh znahm]
Literally, 'May I not know you.' Polish insults and curses, if used by exactly the right person in exactly the right context, can be employed for comic effect and may in fact be hilariously funny, so perhaps it would be fair to include this common and moderate one. However, even this one, with the wrong intonation, and directed towards the wrong person, can of course be devastating.

gównojad
[goov-NOH-jaht]
This put-down, describing a toady, or the person who accepts humiliation and contempt in order to receive privileges, literally translates as 'shit-eater'. Similar to the Dutch expression *de matennaaier*.

motyla noga
[moh-TIL-ah NOH-gah]
A softer curse, literally 'butterfly's leg'.

a pies ci mordę lizał!
[ah P'YES chee MOR-deh LEE-zow]
Literally, 'a dog has licked your gob', this phrase has the strength of "Bugger off!" in English.

Baltic Languages

T he daily curses and insults used in countries of this region, such as Lithuania, Latvia and Estonia, are overwhelmingly peppered with borrowings from Russian – for example, frequently heard in Lithuania are Russian expressions such as *na khui*, 'fuck it', and *blyad* and *kurva*, both meaning 'whore'. As in Poland, those curses that have a somewhat cultural leaning would be considered old-fashioned. Here is a selection of the colourful language of this region.

mine persse!
[MEE-neh PERS-seh] (Estonian)

This means 'Go to the arse!' A very common insult, it actually isn't very cruel. Even so, for the slightly squeamish, it can be said indirectly, translating as 'Go to the good place!' Of course, when heard, the implication is the stronger insult.

kurat!
[KOO-raht] (Estonian)

Literally 'Devil!' Another variation is *kuradi kurat!* 'Devil's devil!' These expressions are very common in everyday conversations in Estonia and are among the most popular curses, used without hesitation in official situations, making it similar to the English "Damn!"

mine metsa!
[MEE-neh MET-sah] (Estonian)
'Go to the wood!' This insult is rather mild and is widely used by children. Adults use other insults such as *idioot*, 'idiot'; *jobu*, 'berk'; and *värdjas*, 'bastard', more regularly.

rupus miltai
[roo-poos mil-tie] (Lithuanian)
A nasty curse phrase which means 'coarse flour'. Another oddity is *nešk muilo* with the force of "get the hell out of here" but the literal meaning 'carry soap'. On the softer side are expressions such as *po galais!* and *po kelmais!* meaning "heck!" and "dash it all!" respectively but translating literally as 'under ends!' and 'under stumps!'

nusišypsosi šaltais dantimis
[noo-see-ship-soh-see shahl-tyce dahn-tee-mees] (Lithuanian)
A traditional Lithuanian threat, this means 'you will smile with cold teeth'. Other traditional curses from northeastern Lithuania are *Trilinkas sau ant kelio triesk*, "Bow yourself threefold and shit on your own way', and *Kad tave žeme prarytu*, "Let the earth swallow you."

cirvis
[TSEER-vees] (Latvian)
The curse words of Latvia also show the rustic influence observed in the Czech and Slovak insults. *Cirvis*, literally 'axe', describes a stupid or idiotic person, while *zirga galva*, 'horse head', and *aitasgalva*, 'sheep head', are other options for your hapless victim.

Yiddish

Y| iddish is a vibrant and expressive language, and this
definitely extends to its repertoire of insults. The *klole*,
or Yiddish curse, is a magnificent thing, prized for
elaborateness and originality; Michael Wex, in his book *Born to
Kvetch*, calls it "a pastime, a form of recreation that lets standard
Yiddish thought and speech run wild." Wex gives an example of
an exchange in which each participant builds on the other's curses:

> *A beyzer gzar zol af dir **kumen**!*
> ('May an evil decree come upon you!')
> ***Kumen** zolstu tsu dayn eybiker **ru**!*
> ('May you come to your eternal rest!')
> ***Ruen** zolstu nisht afile in **keyver**!*
> ('May you find no rest even in the grave!')
> *Zol dir lign in **keyver** der eyver, in di kishkes a lokh
> mit a sheyver!*
> ('May your penis lie in a grave, a hole and
> hernia in your guts!')

Note the virtuoso rhyming in the last imprecation, which
presumably sent the other fellow off in total defeat.

These, of course, are half-playful, however exasperated the
speaker. The Hebrew Bible, however, is full of very unplayful
curses ("Cursed shall you be in the city, and cursed shall you be
in the field . . ."); these biblical curses are known in Yiddish as
toykhekhe, and the name is extended to the more serious Yiddish
curses, of which the most common is *Gey in dr'erd!* ('Go in the
ground', drop dead) and the gravest is *Yemakh shmoy*, 'May his
name be blotted out.' which is straight from the Bible and is often
coupled with the name of Hitler when he is mentioned.

khasene hobn zol er mit di malekhamoves tokhter
[KHAH-seh-neh hob'n zol air mit dee MAH-lekh-a-MO-ves
TOKH-ter]
'He should get married to the daughter of the Angel of Death.'
A classic formulation: it starts off sounding like a blessing, then
comes the zinger.

zalts im in di oygn, fefer im in di noz
[ZAHLTS im in dee OY-g'n, FEH-fer im in dee NOZ]
'Salt in his eyes, pepper in his nose.' Nothing subtle here, just your
basic fling–and-sting.

a meshugenem zol men oysshraybn un dikh araynshraybn
[ah me-SHOOG-eh-nem zol men OYS-shrye-b'n oon DIKH ah-RYNE-
shrye-b'n]
'A crazy person should be discharged and you should be entered
in the register' (of the madhouse). Better a madman should walk
around loose, as long as you get stuck in his place!

got zol oyf im onshikn fun di tsen makes di beste
[got zol oyf im ON-shik'n foon dee TSEHN MAH-kes dee BES-teh]
'God should visit upon him the best of the ten plagues.' See, it's
not so bad – sure, you get a plague, but it's the best one!

got zol in dir nisht fargesn
[got zol in deer NISHT far-GEH-s'n]
'God should never forget about you.' Brilliantly equivocal; it
sounds nice until you realise that it means God's going to be
spending all His time dealing with your constant troubles.

nisht vert ken tsibele
[nisht vairt ken TSEE-beh-leh]
'Not worth an onion', and onions are barely worth anything.
(While we're on the subject, where we say "crocodile tears",
Yiddish talks about *tsibele trern*, 'onion tears'.)

Russian

There is little doubt that Russian culture has become less well-mannered and generally ruder over the years since the end of the Soviet Union. In Soviet times, public opinion on buses or in the street was usually enough to restrain people's behaviour. The drunkard shouting insults and abuse on a bus would be silenced and shamed by fellow passengers; a badly behaved worker might be reported to his employer and fined. But breaking the rules of polite behaviour has become entrenched as a sign of power and being tough, especially among the new rich. Ordinary people now look the other way and put up with public displays of offensive behaviour and language.

There is a long tradition in Russia of children's short humorous verses, *draznilkas*, used to tease and taunt other children and occasionally adults, often with word-play such as *Alesha-balesha, mat' nekhorosha*, 'Alyosha-balyosha, your mother is no good', noted by Halina Weiss in her study of *draznilkas*. The rich culture of teasing and taunts in childhood seems to set Russians up for a rich language of insults and curses as adults. Whether it is appearance, stupidity, clumsiness, sexual prowess (or lack of it), or people's mood and behaviour, Russians have many ways of putting other people down. When stressed or tired, Russians tend to be very direct and insulting to one another. Drivers show great impatience, people trying to get on a bus barge into one another and the person doing the most barging insults the rest, shop assistants and waiters insult customers and tell them to go elsewhere if they comment on poor service.

Anyone interested in the rich topic of Russian vulgarity should seek out *Dermo!: The Real Russian Tolstoy Never Used* by Edward Topol; it's personal rather than scholarly, but Topol is a master of the art and you will learn how to construct a "three-tier

or triple-decker curse", like *khuem pizdanuty mudak*, 'a jerk–off
whacked by a prick'. The chapter "Curses, Oaths, Insults, and
Other Basic Swearing" starts with the basics, like *Poshel ty!*, 'Get
outta here, go to hell!', and *durak*, 'fool' (feminine *dura*), and moves
on to more colourful insults (like *vertikhvostka*, 'ass–swinger', that
is, hussy) and curses (like *Chtob tebya nechistaya sila zabrala!*, 'May
the Dark Force carry you away!').

korova
[kah-ROH-vuh]
'Cow' is a common insult used against a woman, and it's used by
both men and women. It's really meant for a fat woman who
moves around clumsily or a woman who can't do anything
properly, but Russian women tend to be sensitive about their
looks and appearance and are particularly vulnerable to this insult,
often delivered when the person being insulted has left. Just as
widespread is *krysa*, 'rat', to describe mean, cunning and dishonest
behaviour. The ultimate insult, of course, is *blyad*, 'whore', one of
the most common swear words in Russian – it is inserted into
sentences as freely as "fuck(ing)" in English.

dub dubom
[doop doo-BOM]
Dub is 'oak tree'; the phrase could be rendered 'an oak like an oak'
and is used to describe someone behaving like a complete idiot,
someone we may picture as having a thick head and no neck.
Obviously not to be said to his face these days. Older people still
tend to use *kak v shtany nalozhil*, 'as if he had shit in his pants', to
talk about the slow, clumsy person walking with legs wide apart.

krysha poekhala
[KREE-shuh puh-YEH-khuh-luh]
What you can use with children, friends and colleagues when you
think they are being a bit weird and crazy is 'the roof has slid off'.
For those who are even weirder, there's *ne vse doma*, 'not everyone

is at home', and the affectionate *olukh tsarya nebesnogo*, 'God's blockhead', much liked by young people to tell someone he's stupid and silly but not a bad guy. When you start adding *s privyetom* or *s bolshim privyetom*, 'with a hello' or 'with a big hello', the person really could be crazy.

ni rozhi, ni kozhi

[nee ROH-zhee nee KOH-zhee]

Not particularly rude, 'neither skin nor muzzle' is more of a bitchy comment, frequently used by men to other men to show lack of interest in a woman or by women behind another woman's back. *Ne na chto smotret*, 'there's nothing to look at', has similar force, and for something more ironic about a badly dressed woman, people use *chuchelo ogorodnoe*, 'scarecrow', an insult frequently used by children. But for a really bitchy woman-to-woman insult, you probably could not do better than *glista v skafandre*, 'an intestinal worm wearing a diving suit' – and all for being thin and wearing slinky clothes. Hair is often a target for insults and comment. Older people will use *mochalo*, 'bast' (woven wood fibres), to describe hair that looks as if it hasn't been combed for a long time, while younger people will use *mochalka*, 'wisp of bast fibres', for an easy going party girl. If you are making fun of yourself and your rotten hairdo, you'll need *ya u mamy durochka*, 'I am my mother's stupid girl'.

moloko na gubakh ne obsokhlo

[muh-lah-KOH nuh-goo-BAHKH nyih ahp-SOKH-luh]

Older people say 'the milk on his lips has not dried yet' to talk about younger people who show a lack of experience.

A more serious insult along the same lines is *nedonosok*, 'prematurely born child'. You'll often hear it when a young person thought he was experienced enough to do a tough job and didn't listen to advice, and then someone else has to sort out the consequences. The response these days may be *staryi kozyol*, 'old goat'.

tryapka
[TRYAHP-kuh]
There are plenty of insults to be aimed at men. A man who is spineless and hen–pecked may be called a *tryapka*, 'duster'; an alternative is *tyufyak*, the old name for a mattress filled with straw or hay. A *slabak* is a 'weakling' or wimp. Being called a *zayats*, 'hare', used to be a serious accusation of being a coward, but now the sense is closer to "you bunny" and it is used in a more teasing sense, such as before an exam or interview; it's also used for a gatecrasher or someone who gets on a bus without buying a ticket.

lapshu na ushi veshat
[lahp-SHOO NAH-oo-shee VYEH-shut]
A lovely and frequently heard expression is 'to hang a noodle on [someone's] ears', used like the English "to pull the wool over someone's eyes". If the person keeps changing his story and contradicting himself, you might say *sem pyatnits na nedele*, 'there are seven Fridays a week [for him]', a pretty mild put–down, but if it went on and on, you'd end up with *kompostirovat mozgi*, 'to punch [someone's] brain [like a bus ticket]', roughly equivalent to "You're doing my head in!"

v grobu ya tebya vidal!
[vgrah-BOO yah ti-byah vee-DAHL]
A fairly serious curse: 'May I see you in your coffin!' This is more elaborate than the simple expressions *Chtob ty sgorel*, 'May you burn', and *Chtob ty sdokh*, '(May you) drop dead.'

Scandinavian Languages

One of the prime factors in the psychology of medieval Icelanders, and one of the prime engines of the plots of the Norse sagas through which we know them, is the powerful sense of honour which spurred men to win the esteem of their fellows and to avenge any slight, which means that insults play an important role in these stories. For instance, the climax of *Hrafnkel's Saga* is set off when a servant woman runs to tell her master, who through his own stubbornness and pride has been reduced to working for the cousin of a man he had unjustly killed, that the man's brother is passing by the house. She says, "It's true what they used to say, that the older you get the more cowardly you become [*svá ergisk hverr sem eldisk*]. The respect a man gets early on isn't worth much if later he gives it up through dishonour and doesn't have the confidence to take due vengeance." Whereupon her master goes off and takes vengeance.

Iceland also has a long history of invective verse, the most complex of which, *sléttubönd*, is a poem of praise when read normally, but defamatory when read in reverse. The most famous example is this:

Grundar dóma, hvergi hann
hallar réttu máli.
Stundar sóma, aldrei ann
illu pretta táli.

Grounding his judgment in reason, he never
disfavours the right argument.
Pursues honour, never loves
the evil swindles of deception.

In reverse:

Táli pretta illu ann,
aldrei sóma stundar.
Máli réttu hallar hann,
hvergi dóma grundar.

The evil swindles of deception (he) loves,
never pursues honour.
The right argument he disfavours,
never grounding his judgments in reason.

Curses were also important; in *Egil's Saga* the quarrelsome
poet-hero, angry at King Eirik, sets up a *níðstöng* ('scorn-pole'
or 'curse-pole') with a horse's head on its end and curses not only
the king and queen but the *landvættir* ('guardian spirits of the land'),
"so that they may all wander astray and find no place to rest until
they drive King Eirik and Gunnhild from this land."

Religion was also a significant factor after the conversion
of Scandinavia to Christianity around the eleventh century;
even after the recent secularisation of the Nordic countries,
religious curses maintain a strong foothold, as you will see
in the following pages.

Icelandic

A round the year 1000, in the middle of the period the sagas describe, Iceland was converted to Christianity, at first with many compromises but eventually quite thoroughly. Even though modern Iceland is fairly secular, religion plays a strong role in its vulgar language. But of course many curse words and insults have nothing to do with religion, and (as in German) there is a certain amount of focus on the arse and what comes out of it.

skrattinn
[SKRAHT-tin]
This name for the Devil is also a curse word, but there's a euphemistic version, *Skrambinn*, that combines *Skrattinn* with another name for Satan, *Fjandinn*.

helvítis
[HEL-vee-tiss]
Meaning 'hell's', this is a typical thing to say when you hit your thumb with a hammer. Others are *djöfulsins* and *andskotans*, both meaning 'the devil's'.

rassgat
[RAHS-gat]
This word for 'arsehole' can also be used in an affectionate way – a mother might call her child *litla rassgati? mitt*, 'my little arsehole'.

mörður
[MEUR-thuhr]
The name of the main villain in the thirteenth century manuscript *Njál's Saga*, which means 'weasel', is still an insulting

term today, demonstrating the continuity of Icelandic culture.
The character's nickname, *Lyga-Mörður*, is also used as an insult,
meaning 'lying weasel.'

taðskegglingur
[TAHTH-skeg-leen-guhr]
Another term from *Njál's Saga*, this derogatory word for men
whose beards aren't full means 'dried horse shit for beard'; it has
fallen out of fashion along with full beards.

meri
[MEH-rih]
Along with the usual boring insults for women, Icelanders use
the rather charming *meri*, 'filly', with the inevitable appendage
merarsonur, 'son of a filly'.

prumphænsn
[PRUHMP-hine-s'n]
This delightful insult literally means 'fartchicken'.

asni
[AHS-nih]
The literal meaning is 'donkey' but it is used roughly in the same
way "fool" is in English. An expanded version of this insult,
asnaprik, means 'donkeystick'.

ræfill
[RY-vid'l]
Like *rassgat*, this word can be used both pejoratively and
affectionately. It means 'tramp', but when said in a tender voice
the phrase *litli ræfillinn minn*, 'my little tramp', is warm and caring.

Danish

D enmark is a close-knit country with egalitarian values. Its culture of insults is marked by irony and affection. Danes expect others to follow the rules and be courteous, so swift critical comment is likely to fall on those who fail to conform or who speak before they think. There is also a strong streak of prejudice of Copenhagen dwellers towards those who are less fortunate and live in provincial Denmark.

at ligne en hængt kat
[ahd ligh-nuh en hengd kahd]

Appearance is important in Denmark – not surprising for a country which values design so highly. It's important to look your best, and someone who doesn't might hear the expression 'to look like a hanged cat'. Actually, you would probably say this only to someone you know very well, since it would be very insulting indeed to say it to someone's face. Equivalent, and just like the English, is *at ligne en sæk kartofler*, 'to look like a sack of potatoes'.

du har jord i hovedet
[doo hahr YOR ee HOH-vuh-dhuhd]

'You have dirt in your head.' Danes do not suffer fools gladly and will be happy to tell you that you are completely wrong – though this insult is on the strong side. There are plenty of other expressions to denigrate people who are not particularly bright, such as *Hun stod ikke forrest i køen, da der blev uddelt hjerner*, 'She was not at the front of the queue when they handed out brains', and

Han er ikke den skarpeste kniv i skuffen, 'He is not the sharpest knife in the drawer.' *Kyllingehjerne,* 'chicken brain,' is also a strong put-down which needs no translation. Then there is *Han er ikke født igår,* 'He was not born yesterday', which may be used to describe someone clever but is more often used ironically as a put-down.

en tørvetriller
[en TEUR-vuh-tril-er]
This is difficult to translate but is roughly equivalent to "party-pooper", a person who is not only boring but can ruin a party by spoiling the mood.

en gammel heks
[en gah-muhl hegs]
Danes have a battery of insults for women; this one means 'an old witch'. For older women you can also use *havgasse,* 'old witch', while those with loose tongues risk being told that they are *en sladderkælling,* 'a gossiping bitch'.

et pernippengryn
[ed pair-NIP-puhn-grewn]
Well nigh impossible to translate and well suited to the Danes' laid-back culture, this put-down is used for someone overly anal or obsessed with unimportant things. Danes use it to get others to lighten up, and it is usually used with some affection rather than in an insulting way. Another phrase, aimed at men, is *slapsvans,* 'weak queer'. This really speaks for itself, and again it can be used either as a strong insult to expose someone's weakness in doing physical tasks or in a joking, ironic way in front of the person. An alternative is the childish *gummi-tarzan,* 'rubber Tarzan'.

at køre som en brækket arm
[ahd keur-uh som en brag-uhd ahrm]
Try out 'to drive like a broken arm' in English and see what the reactions are. Not particularly strong in Danish, even jokey at times, it is used to try and curb bad or fast driving.

Swedish

To English speakers, the Swedish language might seem very poor in insults and curses, and it might be fair to say that they are not a very developed part of Swedish language and culture. The Swedes certainly don't do subtle verbal insults. Interruption is probably the most common way of annoying someone, together with forgetting a person's name and pretending not to hear what they are saying. Dry understatement also tends to work. However, things can suddenly heat up, going directly to shouting with streams of obscenities. It does, however, take quite a lot to push a grown-up Swede to this. These days you are likely, especially with young people, to hear English curses straight out of American movies.

åsnan mellan två hötappar
[OS-nahn meh-lahn tvoh HEU-tah-pahr]
There is still a range of quaint rural expressions in Sweden, which until recently was largely agricultural. An example like 'a donkey between two stacks of hay' is used against someone who cannot make up his mind, but you won't hear it used often by people under fifty. There are lots of standard ones such as *dum som en gås*, 'stupid as a goose'; *tjock som en gris*, 'fat as a pig'; and *envis som en åsna*, 'stubborn as a donkey', that are also only used by older people these days. More likely today is that you'll hear a swear word plus whatever you would like to emphasise. *Du är helt djävla dum i huvudet*, 'You are fucking stupid', has largely replaced *dum som en gås*, except in families with young children. The word *djävla* (usually pronounced YEV-lah) literally means 'devilish' but has more the impact of the English "fucking".

inte rent mjöl i påsen
[IN-tuh rent myeul ee POH-suhn]
Another farm expression that has survived, 'not pure flour in the sack', is still commonly used to describe someone as a crook.

stockholmsfasoner
[STOK-holms-fah-soh-ner]
The tension between the city and countryside is still alive and well. If you are pretentious and snobbish in your behaviour, you may be put down by being accused of having 'Stockholm manners', while the slick city dweller may respond with *bondtölp*, 'farm boy', suggesting that his interlocutor is unsophisticated and lacks manners.

din bil är skitful!
[deen beel air SHIT-fool]
Better take care of your car, or you may be told, 'Your car is shit-ugly!' The most widely used swear word in Swedish is probably *skit*, 'shit'. It's not particularly offensive on its own, but it tends to get added as a reinforcement to almost anything, for example *Han är skitstor*, 'He's shit-big', that is, really big; another common use is in *skitsnack*, 'shit-talk', "bullshit".

ta mig fan!
[tah may fahn]
Another example of religion-based cursing: 'The devil take me!' is used like the English "Dammit!" Similarly, *Det var som fan*, 'It was like the devil', matches up with "God damn it!" or "Bloody hell!" Another word for the devil, *satan*, is used as a stand-alone exclamation parallel to "Shit!" or in the

possessive, *satans*, in sentences like *Jag har haft en satans dag!*, 'I've had a devil's day' (that is, "a hell of a day"). And *Dra åt helvete!*, literally 'go to hell', is much stronger in Sweden, equivalent to "Fuck off!" Even though Sweden is quite a secular country, religious curses are still some of the strongest available.

kyss mig i arslet!
[shyus may ee AHRS-luht]
Just like English-speakers, the Swedes are fond of saying 'Kiss my arse!'

har du piss i huvudet, eller?
[hahr due PISS ee HUE-vue-duht, eh-ler]
If someone cuts you off or spills his drink on you, you can ask him 'Have you got piss in your head, or what?'

noll-åtta
[nool OT-tah]
An insult that is directed at a person from Stockholm; another that shows the tension between city and country, it originates from the area code for the city, 08.

Norwegian

L ike other Scandinavian languages, Norwegian relies heavily on religion for many of its basic swear words; the culture may have become secularised, but not the cussing! Words for 'devil' carry far more clout than an English-speaker would expect. But there are, of course, the usual complement of more earthly forms of swearing, based on the lower portions of the human anatomy.

There's a great deal of dialectical difference in Norway; similarly, there are regional differences in swearing. The far north in particular is proud of the colour, inventiveness and richness of its swearing. In particular, *hestkuk*, 'horse cock', is a well-known insult native to the north (Nordland, Troms and Finnmark); it can be strengthened as *forpulte hestkuk*, 'fucking horse cock', with *forpulte* derived from *pule*, 'to fuck'.

faen
[FAH-uhn]
This word for 'devil', the popular pronunciation (often shortened still further to just *fan*) of the official word *fanden*, is the foundation stone of much Norwegian swearing; it occurs by itself as an exclamation and as part of expressions such as *faen i helvete*, 'the devil and hell' ("God damn it!"); *faen er løs*, 'the devil is loose' ("There'll be hell to pay!"); *faen til kar*, 'a hell of a guy'; and *hva faen vil du?*, 'What the hell do you want?'

jævla or *jævlig*
[YEV-lah, YEV-lee]
These words, literally 'devilish' (from *djevel*, 'devil'), have an even greater force than *faen*, and are roughly equivalent to the English "fucking". They can be neutral (*jævlig stor*, 'damn big') or openly

offensive: the occasional rivalry with the neighbours to the east is expressed with the oft-muttered *jævla svenske*, 'fucking Swede!'

dra til helvete!
[drah til HEL-ve-te]
'Go to hell' is pretty much universal. A nice euphemism is *Dra dit pepper`n gror!*, 'Go where the pepper grows!'

kyss meg i ræva!
[chews may ee RAV-ah]
This means 'Kiss my arse!'; a slightly more polite version is *Kyss meg bak!* 'Kiss my backside!' Another word for 'arse' is *rass*, which is historically the same word as the English one – the *r* and *a* have simply gotten switched around. And just as in English, they say *rasshøl*, 'arsehole'.

pikk
[pik]
This word for 'prick, cock' sounds a little childish and is not a particularly effective insult by itself, but combined with *tryne*, 'snout, face', you get *pikktryne*, 'dickface', which carries more clout. The Norwegian version of British comedian Richard Herring's one-man show, *Talking Cock* (a male answer to the *Vagina Monologues*), is called *Pikk Preik*, 'prick chat/nonsense'.

fitte
[FIT-te]
The Norwegian word for 'cunt' is an especially popular insult among the young, who perhaps overuse it. The car released by Honda as the Fit was originally going to be called Fitta, but it was renamed when they realised the unfortunate connotations this would carry in Scandinavia; just to make sure, in Europe it's called the Honda Jazz.

Finnish

I nsults in Finnish often take the form of wise sayings rather than the more direct face-to-face insults of other languages and cultures. Like the other Nordic peoples, Finns are strong on honesty, directness and speaking only after thinking. Transgressions may come in for swift verbal punishment.

Finnish is not a culture known for its wit, and laughing too much may be frowned on as a sign of immaturity and lack of seriousness. There's a nasty put-down: *Tulee se mies räkänokastakin, vaan ei tyhjän naurajasta*, 'Even the one with the snotty nose grows up to be a man, but not the one who laughs for nothing.'

Finns like playing with sounds in their insults, such as *ruma kuin petolinnun perse*, 'ugly like the backside of a vulture' and the warning against ridiculing others, *Pilkka käy oman nilkkaan*, 'If you ridicule someone it will hit you on your own ankle', with the assonance of *pilkka* and *nilkka*. Or the humorous rather than insulting *niin pihi, että pieraiseekin sisäänpäin*, 'so mean that (s)he even farts inwards'.

tyhmä kuin (vasemman jalan) saapas
[TEWHH-ma KOO-in (VAH-sem-mahn YAH-lahn) SAH-pahs]
There are plenty of the usual insults, too, especially those about stupidity such as 'thick as a (left-legged) boot'; the best of these are probably *tulee iltajunassa*, 'coming home with the evening train', for the slow-witted and always last to get the idea, and *Meitä on moneen junaan, ja moni jää vielä asemalle*, 'We have many trains, some stay at the station', for someone doing something utterly stupid. But what are we to make of *Tukka ja järki eivät pysy samassa päässä*, 'Hair and the ability to think won't grow on the same head'? It may sound nasty, but it is often used in a positive way: you may be bald, but at least you're smart. Similarly, *Siinä*

miehessä ei seiso muu kuin järki,
'The only thing stiff in him
is his mind', which is used
to describe someone's
low intellect more than
their sexual ability.

vain rumat ne vaatteilla koreilee
[VAH-in ROO-maht neh VAHT-teh-il-lah KOH-reh-ee-lay]
A flamboyant dresser may be
told 'only the ugly need to
decorate themselves with
clothes'. This goes further than
just dressing – it enshrines the
Finnish virtue of modesty.

tarpeeton kuin nunnan nännit
[TAHR-pay-tohn KOO-in NOON-nahn NAN-nit]
The Finns being a striving, generally hard-working and well-educated people, there are plenty of insults and put-downs for the lazy, less able, or less well organised, such as 'as useless as a nun's nipples'. Someone full of bright but impractical ideas may be labelled a *serpentini* – the name given to party streamers that pop out, stream and die away. In the end, though, the key to Finnish insults lies in truth. In many cultures, the force of an insult may lie in its lack of truth, but in Finnish culture, where truth is what matters, probably the worst insult of the lot is to be called *epäluotettava*, 'unreliable'.

perkele
[PAIR-keh-leh]
This most famous of Finnish curses is a term for the devil, derived from the ancient god of fire, thunder and warriors, and then co-opted by Christianity. An alternative term for 'devil', also used as a

curse, is *saatana*. Finns (both men and women) will invoke God when cursing mildly, too. *Herra jestäs*, 'Good God!', is to be heard frequently at times of stress or, if someone is feeling really frustrated, *Herra Jumala* (literally 'Lord God', but probably closer to "Dear God in Heaven!" in strength) or *Jumalauta*, a combination of *jumala* and *auta*, 'help', though the closest English is probably "God damn it!" rather than "God help me!"

vittu
[VIT-too]

This ancient word for 'cunt' has been called the most overused word in Finnish; particularly among young people, it can be used several times in a sentence, much like "fuck" in English. Besides occurring on its own, it is used as an intensifier (*vitun äpärä*, "fucking bastard") and is part of many expressions, such as *Ja vitut!*, which could be rendered "The fuck you say!" or "Bullshit!", and *Voi vittu!* "Oh, fuck!" A fine expression of complete disgust is *Voi vittujen kevät ja kyrpien takatalvi!*, literally 'the spring of cunts and the late winter of dicks' but loosely translatable as "Oh, fucking shit!"

hemmetti
[HEM-met-tee]

A mild curse, meaning 'darn' or 'hell', that can safely be used in front of one's granny.

Middle Eastern Languages

A s the cradle of civilisation, the Middle East has some of the oldest curses as well as the oldest writing; see the introduction to the Ancient Languages section for examples from Sumer and Egypt. Since those days, the region has been shaped first by the Greco-Roman and Persian imperial civilisations and then by the coming of Islam, which brought a whole new set of values as well as the Arabic language, rich in curses as in other sorts of vocabulary.

The cultural importance of honour in the region is immense, and is the basis for a large range of curses and insults. To insult a man's family, particularly his female relatives, is a very serious thing, and the word *ummak*, 'your mother', features prominently in Arabic curses. The most basic of these is probably *qus ummak*, 'your mother's cunt', and because of the scarcity of Hebrew curses, it is common in Israeli use as well, as are many other

Arabic curses. A well-known Israeli comedy sketch illustrates the history of successive waves of immigrants coming to regard themselves as locals and despising the next wave to arrive, the Polish Jews looking down on the Germans and the latter on the Yemenites, each expressing its scorn with the Palestinian Arabic expression *Il'an babur illi jabak*, 'Curse the ship that brought you', picked up by the first Zionist arrivals from the local Arabs.

Russian is another source of Israeli curses. Native Israeli taxi drivers can be heard to shout things like *yob tvoyu mat!*, 'fuck your mother!', and the related *ebyona mat* (literally 'fucked mother', but used like "dammit!" or "I'll be damned!") has been fully naturalised as *kibinimat*, which many Israelis don't even realise is originally Russian.

One ancient fear in the region is that of the "evil eye" – Arabic *ayn hasad*, 'eye of envy' (or simply *al-ayn*, 'the eye'), Turkish *nazar*, 'look, glance' or *kem göz*, 'evil eye'. And the Quran refers to "those who blow upon knots" as practicing some sort of magic curse, to be avoided by taking refuge in God.

Here's a nice anecdote on the importance of being careful how you curse, from Yasir Suleiman's book *Language and Identity in the Middle East and North Africa*:

A Libyan and a Tunisian are walking down the street in Tunis. They see a beautiful young lady. The Tunisian compliments her with a *piropo* [a Spanish term for a flirtatious compliment to a woman]: *yil'an bu-z-zin* (freely translatable as 'Damn! Aren't you beautiful!' but literally, 'Damn the father of [this] beauty', *zin*, which is also the name of the Tunisian president, Zine El Abidine Ben Ali). Upon returning to Libya and seeing a beautiful young lady walking down the street, the Libyan calls out to her, 'Damn the father of Gaddafi!' and is hauled away to prison.

Arabic

T he famous tenth-century Arabic poet al-Mutanabbi wrote a satirical poem that ended up costing him his life because of its biting insults. A group of people are walking along, al-Mutanabbi among them, when Daba Ibn Fatik al-Asadi, a highwayman, tries to rob them. The highwayman is chased off and runs to take shelter in a fortified tower. From here, he peeps out of one of the windows and shouts abuse at his pursuers. On the spot, al-Mutanabbi composed the satire against him, with the famous line:

> *Ya atyab el nas nafsan*
> *Wa alyan al nas rukba*

> You are the kindest of all people
> with the softest of knees.

Now, this may be lost on most readers, but those who understand Arabic will recognise the insult implied in the "softest of knees" reference. This is a veiled allusion to being homosexual. As they say, it would be better to kill a Bedouin Arab than insult him with an accusation of homosexuality.

On the whole, it is wise to avoid using insults in Arabic. Mothers, sisters and daughters are strictly off-limits, of course, and even between friends, the use of jokey insults such as *ya khayib*, "poof", has to be approached very cautiously.

jahsh
[JAH-huhsh]
Classical Arabic has a long tradition of subtle, witty and clever insults in prose and poetry; however, contemporary spoken Arabic

tends to be much more direct and abusive in its use of insults and curses. Take stupidity, for example. A father, seeing his son being stupid or misbehaving, is likely to call him *jahsh*, 'little donkey', while a servant dropping something, or some careless driving, may earn *hamar*, 'donkey'. Of course, there are some interesting regional differences. In Morocco, the local form of 'little donkey', *hamir*, may be used as a term of affection and tolerance when things go wrong.

kalb
[kalb]
Probably the ultimate insult in Arabic is to call someone *kalb* 'dog'. While this might seem odd to the Western ear, the origin of this term is in Islamic culture, where the dog is described as being impure and unclean. If a dog goes into the kitchen and touches something, you are supposed to wash what has been touched

---

airi fik
[EYE-ree fik]
A very offensive, grave insult meaning 'my dick in you' may accompany this rude gesture, which is a sexual mime. Anything that has a sexual connotation in Arabic societies is considered a very severe insult and is only used in the most extreme and heated circumstances.

Gesture
The fingers are splayed in a reverse V-sign and rubbed either side of the nose.

seven times. *Kalb* is hurled at offending drivers in road rage and is used to pay back really bad behaviour. Such occasions might be when you have been cheated out of some money or when someone has shown gross disrespect.

thawr Allah fi birsimihi
[thowr uhl-LAH fee beer-SEE-mee-hee]
This insult will usually produce a smile. Literally meaning 'a bull belonging to God in clover', it's an image of a bull on a farm just eating lush grass and oblivious to the danger that he is being fattened up to provide meat. It is used of people who seem to be unaware of what's going on around them or who lack drive and ambition. A parent may use it about a self-absorbed child, or an employer may use it about an employee who is not performing well. Some other neat insults for those who are either weak or pretty useless at whatever they do are *alanz takul 'ashah*, 'God can make off with his supper', and if you are clumsy, erratic and awkward, *el jamal elauraq*, 'an awkward camel running'.

tali fawq rasi
[TAH-lee fowk RAH-see]
Literally 'you're climbing on my head', this insult has a wide range of meanings depending on the context. It can simply mean "you're getting on my nerves" or "you're causing me a lot of inconvenience". But it can also be used of someone who is trying to take advantage of you or who has gone too far and needs to be put down a bit. Arabic-speaking societies are still predominantly hierarchical, so someone who has strayed out of their position may be at the receiving end or may hear instead the phrase *nakikhun awdajhi*, 'puffed up cheeks', for thinking themselves more than they really are.

Turkish

W atch your step with insults in Turkey. As in many other countries, insulting the wrong person at the wrong time and place, however inadvertently and unintentionally, could cost you your life. However, there are contexts where the most foul-mouthed insults are permitted – for example, football games. Players are permitted to exchange the grossest insults about their respective mothers and sisters and the sexual acts they might perform on them, all without retribution or the threat of being killed.

City people in Turkey tell stories about the insult culture of those in rural areas, particularly Anatolia, where there is a village famed for its ritualised exchanges of insults. Two women will take themselves off to hilltops within shouting distance of one another and hurl insults, accompanied by gestures, and often using the potential power of male members of the family to do harm to the other: *Kocam seni becersin*, 'My husband should fuck you.' Within such a culture, oral literature is strong, and such ritualised insults provide for the expression of feelings in a structured way. The potential for physical violence is defused through verbal violence, as it were.

Life is simple in rural areas and insults tend to be of the direct, unkind, physical variety: *şişko*, 'fat'; *cılız*, 'puny'; *topal*, 'crippled'; *sağir*, 'deaf'; *sırık*, 'pole' (meaning "beanpole", very tall person); *cüce*, 'dwarf', highlighting physical deformity or difference. It is in rural Turkey (and among the urban working class) that you'll still find the old curses, such as *Allah canini alsin*, 'Allah should take your soul', and *Allah belani versin*, 'Allah should give you trouble.'

muhallebi çocuğu
[moo-hahl-leh-BEE choh-joo-OO]
This means 'child of pudding' and refers to a person who has had life too easy.

orospu
[oh-rohs-POO]
To say that the culture of insulting is complex is an understatement. Take the word *orospu*, 'whore'. In most contexts, it would be highly insulting to use it, while within small female peer groups in villages, *kaltak*, 'slut', and even *kevase*, 'prostitute', may be quite okay. In a country where honour killings still take place in rural areas, the use of the very offensive phrase *orospu çocuğu*, 'child of a whore', outside the permitted context might be a slur on a family's honour and would require retribution by a male member of the family to regain the family's "face".

eşşoğlu eşek
[ESH-oh-loo eh-SHEK]
The insult you are most likely to hear in Istanbul is 'son of a donkey'; car drivers routinely call one another this. And in similar vein, you'll probably hear *hıyar* (literally 'cucumber', but meaning "jerk" or "arsehole") and often used in the phrase *Hıyar gibi adam*, 'That guy's an arsehole.'

kancık
[kahn-JIHK]
Meaning 'bitch, female animal', this is a strong insult that someone isn't a real man, though it can be used in a humorous way.

Persian

I ran has had a literate civilisation for thousands of years, and Persian has an ancient tradition of polite, not to say obsequious, speech. Perfectly ordinary correspondence can involve salutations like "May I be sacrificed to you" and "I drown your face with my kisses from afar." But the language also, needless to say, makes room for less flattering forms of speech. It can employ the usual repertoire of unseemly body parts and actions (including such arcane references as "the left testicle of the disciple Abbas's horse"), but it can also disguise them with the placeholder word *folaan*, 'such-and-such, so-and-so,' which allows the recipient to replace it with whatever insult the imagination can supply, whether obscene or rococo. The following is a sampler of some of the sayings and metaphors used to suggest various human failings.

khaane taarik kon va kooche roshan kon
[khawneh taw-REEK kon va koocheh ro-SHAN kon]
We all know people who are nice as pie when they're out in public but turn mean when they're with their family; in such cases, the phrase in Persian is 'the darkness of the home, the light of the street.'

khoroos-e bi-mahal
[kho-ROOS-eh BEE-ma-hal]
It might have been a good thing to do . . . some other time! In Persian, they call that an 'untimely cock's crow'.

kharchang va ghurbaaghe neveshtan
[khar-CHANGG va koor-baw-GHEH neh-vesh-tan]
When we can't make out someone's handwriting, we may mutter

about "chicken scratch"; in Persian they say 'to write like crab and frog'.

mesl-e gaav khordan
[mes-leh GAWV khor-dan]
We say a greedy person eats like a pig; in Persian, it's 'to eat like a cow'.

khers-e gonde
[khers-eh gon-DEH]
Those of unusual girth have to put up with unflattering descriptions in many societies; in Persian, they're called 'big bear'.

div-e dajaal
[DEEV-eh da-JAWL]
And then there are those who don't meet the prevailing standards of beauty; "ugly as sin" is along the same lines as the Persian 'deceiver devil'.

deraaz-e bad ghavaare
[de-rawz-eh bad ka-vaw-REH]
Tall can be good, but too tall is 'long and ill-shaped'.

khar tu khar
[khar too KHAR]
When a situation is completely disorganised, utter chaos, Persian calls it 'donkey over donkey.' Donkeys feature in other insults, for example *kor-e khar*, 'son of a donkey'; in olden times, a traditional way to put a social inferior in his place if he spoke without having been addressed was to ask him *Kharat be chand?*, or 'How much for your donkey?'

gur be guri
[goor beh goo-ree]
To wish that someone not rest in peace, Persians can say 'from grave to grave': *Haaji gur be guri!* 'May Haji not rest in peace!'

pedar sokhteh!
[peh-DAR sohkh-TEH]
The fires of hell feature in Persian cursing; this common insult means 'burned father', and a traditional curse is *aatesh be jaanat biyoftad*, 'may your soul catch fire!' But burning doesn't have to be so drastic – the Persian equivalent of having your leg pulled is *damaa sokhteh*, '[you got your] nose burned'.

khaak bar sar!
[KHAWK bar sar]
You can damn something or someone by saying 'dust/earth on [its/his] head'; to address it to someone directly, you say *khaak bar saret*, 'dust on your head'.

ghasamat kamarat-raa bezanad!
[ka-SAM-at ka-MAR-at-raw BEH-za-nad]
If you think someone's lying to you, 'May your oath strike your waist/loins' is a good old-fashioned way of telling them off. An alternative is *Qasamat-raa bebinam yaa dom-e khorus-raa?* 'Should I see [that is, believe] your oath or the cock's tail [sticking out of your pocket, proof of falsehood and robbery]?' Which of course brings to mind Groucho Marx's "Who are you going to believe, me or your own eyes?"

African
Languages

A frica, and particularly South Africa, has a rich culture of insults and curses. In South Africa, as in many countries, using different styles of speech for insults is common but it can be taken to its ultimate as English, Afrikaans, Xhosa and Zulu are all used as invective. There are also a host of racial insults, probably the largest category. One thing to note is that as the continent is largely Christian, the invective, while common, is even more taboo than in other cultures – to be clear, these insults are not used or appreciated in polite society.

rooinek
[ROY-nek] (Afrikaans)
Afrikaans for 'red–neck', but not in the American "trailer trash" sense. It is a derogatory term for white English–speaking people, based on the fact that when they experience prolonged exposure to the harsh African sun, their pasty white skin turns blistering red.

soutpiel or soutie
[SOHT-peel, SOH-tee] (Afrikaans)
This Afrikaans insult for white English–speaking people literally translates as 'salt–penis', metaphorically derived from the notion that English settlers in South Africa kept one foot in Africa and one in Europe, with the result that their genitals dangled in the sea, washed by salt water. This is more offensive than rooinek.

rockspider
(South African English)

This is an English–speaker's insult for Afrikaners, dating from the Anglo–Boer War, where the popular conception had them fleeing away from combat like spiders scurrying under rocks.

jy was uit jou ma se gat gebore want sy so besig was om te naai
[yay vahs oeyt yoh MAH-suh KHAHT khuh-BOH-ruh vahnt say soh BEE-suhkh vahs om tuh NYE] (Afrikaans)

'You were born out of your mother's anus because she was so busy fucking (at the time).' I particularly enjoy this rather crass Afrikaans insult, once hurled randomly at a friend of mine by some construction workers, but apparently in fairly wide circulation. Needless to say, this is extremely rude.

jou ma se poes
[yoh MAH-suh POOS] (Afrikaans)

'Your mother's vagina'. This is a ubiquitous default expression of frustration or dislike which originated with the "Cape Coloured" Afrikaans-speaking population but has since spread widely, and is certainly the Afrikaans insult in widest circulation, transcending linguistic borders. It not only conveys a sense of utter disgust, anger, or dismay, but also has come to be a characterisation of an entire racial group. White or more "respectable" Afrikaans tends to use a more contemporary, less harsh, more Dutch Reformed version, *jou ma se e-pos*, said, of course, in a "Coloured" accent for some flair and a sense of authenticity. (*E-pos* is Afrikaans for 'e-mail'; so, literally, 'your mother's e-mail'.) There are many extensions of this insult, such as *jou ma se verlepte double-adaptor*, 'your mother's drooping/crumpled double-adaptor' or, less euphemistically, "your mother's sloppy vagina"). This is usually produced in a "Cape Coloured" accent, the last word pronounced *double-edeptor*, so that it rhymes.

moffie

[MOH-fee] (Afrikaans)

Afrikaans insults are often derogatory remarks about manhood, such as this one meaning 'weak, effeminate', which has the sense of being camp and homosexual. The origin of this word is uncertain. It may have come from livestock farming, where being *moffie* or *mof* is the result of breeding from imported stock. It is widely used by English-speakers. There's also the extension *koffie-moffie*, a male air steward – by implication, usually gay.

umsunu ka nyoko

[oom-SOO-noo kah NYOH-koh] (Xhosa)

Xhosa is rich in crude and offensive but ultimately humorous insults such as this one, meaning 'your mother's arse'; others are *srhama sakho*, 'a skid-mark on underwear'; *undi qhela ngama nqate omsunu ka nyoko*, 'the excess fat skin around your mother's rectum.

undi qhela uboya wo-nodoli

[oon-dee KEH-lah oo-BOY-ah woh-noh-DOH-lee] (Xhosa)

For something a little less offensive and less masculine, Xhosa offers the relatively mild insult 'as fickle as doll's hair': *undi qhela uboya wo-nodoli* (mocking somebody's fake hair extensions).

tsotsi

[TSOH-tsee] (Sesotho)

This is a Sesotho slang word for a thug. Combined with *taal*, the Afrikaans word for 'language', *Tsotsitaal* or *isiCamtho* is pidgin mainly spoken in townships such as Soweto.

anu ofia nzuzu ka gi nma

[ah-noo oh-fee-ah n'zoo-zoo kah ghee nn-mah] (Igbo)

Igbo, one of the languages of Nigeria, has some colourful insults. This one, while not a particularly strong insult, still gets the point across: 'a useless and foolish animal is better than you'.

otoro gba gbue kwa gi

[oh-toh-roh bah boo-eh kwah gee] (Igbo)
An Igbo curse, which is not much stronger but certainly paints
a more disturbing picture, this phrase means, 'may you die of
uncontrollable running stomach'. Death seems to be rained down
indiscriminately on the heads of your enemies and you may say
egbe enu igwe gha wa kwa gi isi, 'May thunder blast your head'
or *egbe gbarie kwa gi isi*, 'Let a gun blow your head to pieces.'

ima abanatara onwe gi uru na ndu a

[ee-mah ah-bah-nah-tah-rah on-weh ghee oo-roo nah n'doo ah]
(Igbo)
If calling down a curse of death isn't quite your style, you can go
on the attack in this life as well with *ima abanatara onwe gi uru na
ndu a*, 'You will never amount to anything good in life.'

mwazirifu

[mwah-zee-REE-foo] (Swahili)
Swahili culture is extremely private and personal relationships
are very rarely spoken of. It follows then, that if you are in the
position to insult someone, then you know too much about the
life and activities of the insulted and his or her family. If you speak
openly about the shameful things of the family, you will be
insulted yourself with this word *mwazirifu*, literally 'exposer'.

sabasi

[sah-BAH-see] (Swahili)
The closest English counterpart to this insult is "troublemaker"
or "tale-bearer". Going hand-in-hand with *mwazirifu*, a *sabasi*
causes ill-will and bad feeling among people by telling tales
and spreading gossip.

Asian Languages

T he popular image of Asia involves ancient civilisations and cultures built on respect and fear of the loss of face, with occasional reference to Confucianism. There is, of course, some truth to this, as there is to most cultural generalisations, but it might lead one to think these nations were deficient in the kind of language this book features. Nothing could be farther from the truth!

There are, of course, ritualised forms of politeness, as in most societies, and the foreigner will quite properly be advised to observe them, but if you get out where people mingle informally, in markets and crowded buses and busy intersections, you are likely to hear forms of speech they don't tell you about in an introductory language course. In China you will hear *ta ma de!* "dammit!" and *jiba ren*, 'bastard, jerk', and even *cao ni ma!* 'fuck your mother!'; in Japan, the rudeness will often consist of impolite verbal forms (for example, *shite yagaru* 'is doing' instead of the polite *shite imasu*) and pronouns (*temae* for 'you' – especially in its colloquial pronunciation *temee* – is so aggressive it has been likened to saying "Oi! Arsehole!"), but there are also expletives like *chikushou* (comparable to "Damn!" or "Shit!") and *baka*, 'idiot' (often extended to *bakayarou*), which Peter Constantine (in his invaluable *Japanese Street Slang*) calls "the most popular Japanese swear word". Korean curse words can depend heavily on context; the frequently used *seki(-ya)* or *sekkya*, for example, literally 'young of an animal', can be quite inoffensive or can be a serious insult. A nice traditional Korean curse is *yeombyeonghal nom*, 'person who will die of the plague'; a more pungent modern one is *dahk daegori*, 'chicken head'. And calling someone *michin*, 'crazy', is a good way to start a fight.

Many Chinese speakers have a sense that certain dialects are easier or more effective for swearing than others; both Shanghainese and Cantonese are sometimes thought better than Mandarin for that purpose. Of course, Beijingers curse as much as anybody else, but there is a feeling that other dialects are earthier, perhaps because Mandarin is a second language for so many and learned in a formal setting.

In the Indian subcontinent, as in many traditional cultures, family is all-important, and a common insult is to call a man "brother-in-law", because it implies that you have slept with his sister; likewise, incest is a frequent theme (for example, the Hindi *bhen-chhod*, 'sister-fucker'). But there are also amusing, slangy insults like *angootha chhaap*, 'thumbs up', which describes illiterate people who place thumb marks on documents in lieu of signatures, and (in Mumbai slang) "Bombay docks", used for someone with bad body odour. And in Bengali, the word *alu*, 'potato', is also slang for 'testicle', and someone who behaves badly because of lust ("thinking with his dick") may either hear or use the phrase *alur dosh*, 'the fault of the testicles'. Interestingly, the great sixteenth-century Mughal emperor Akbar is known to have used a Hindustani curse word; before killing a traitor, he called him *ya gandu*, 'you catamite!'

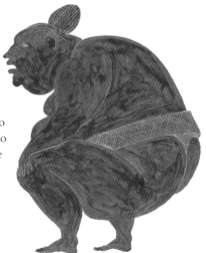

In the inner depths of Asia, Mongolians have so few serious curse words of their own that they have to import Russian ones; left to their own devices, Mongolians who hit their thumb with a hammer are likely to holler *huur*, 'carrion!'

Chinese

There is a story that Fu Bi, an eleventh-century Chinese statesman, had an effective way of dealing with people who directed curses at him. At first he would ignore them. If someone called his attention to the cursing, he would say that it must be intended for someone else. If he was told, "He's cursing you by name," he would respond that there were many people called Fu Bi in China. By this time, the curser generally gave up and went away. Whether or not this actually worked, it's clear the Chinese have been cursing for a long time.

As is common around the world, the Chinese frequently attack their victim via the latter's mother; "(I) fuck(ed) your mother's cunt" is frequently heard in both the Mandarin (*cao ni ma ge bi*) and Cantonese (*diu nei lou mou hai*) versions, and an abbreviated and depersonalised form, *ta ma de*, 'his/its mother's', is the normal thing to holler when you stub your toe. (The famous author Lu Xun wrote an entire essay on this expression.) More specific to China is the subject of turtles. The turtle has represented longevity and wisdom in China at least since the Han Dynasty, but it also has sexual connotations (sometimes explained by the resemblance of the turtle's head and neck to the human penis – *gui tou*, 'turtle's head', is a euphemism for penis). At any rate, the turtle is a symbol of cuckoldry, so the insult *wang ba dan*, 'turtle's egg', implies "son of a cuckolded father." And dogs also turn up frequently: *gou pi*, 'dog's fart', is the Chinese equivalent of "bullshit," and a collision between cars may produce an outburst like *Cao ni de ye! Xia le gou yan, shi bu shi?* 'Fuck your uncle! You're blind in your dog eyes, aren't you?'

In the last ten years, the situation may have changed. Some say that insults have become subtler and more indirect and that many people prefer using apparently positive sayings to insult others.

As a result, you may think you are being praised or flattered, but the sentence contains a negative word which has the same pronunciation as the positive word you thought was intended. There are some examples among the following Mandarin expressions.

yi qie xiang qian kan
[yee chyeh shyahng chyen kahn]
The saying 'You should look forward' is used to encourage people. But *qian* can mean both 'forward' and 'money', so the underlying meaning can be 'you look at the money' – that is, you won't help out unless you're being paid.

wan jin you
[wahn jin yoh]
This is a balm for treating headaches, scalds and other minor ailments; as an expression it can be used with the sense of "Jack of all trades and master of none". There are some other similar put-downs, such as *lin zhen mo dao, bu kai ye guang*, 'the knife is not sharp (enough), but it shines'; if you're prone to hasty last-minute work, you may well be at the receiving end of this.

di zhong hai
[dee jong hie]
'The sea in the middle of lands' (that is, the Mediterranean) is a lovely image for someone who is bald. There are other images describing people's appearance; for instance, large women may be called *you tong*, 'pillar box', or even *wan dun ju lun*, 'ten-thousand-ton ocean-going ship'.

da tou cangying
[dah toh tsang-ying]
There are many ways of telling people that they are stupid; someone who is acting without a good plan or purpose can be called a 'big-headed fly'. Another is *naozi jin shui le*, 'the water has come into your brain', for someone who is stupid and clumsy – quite strong unless you are just joking. Then there's *dai ruo muji* 'dumb as a wooden chicken'. One of the most curious insults of this type is *er bai wu*, which literally means 'two hundred and fifty'; it is not clear why this number came to refer to a stupid person. One theory involves an ancient unit of currency, called a *diao*, representing a thousand copper coins; a modest person might call himself a *ban diao zi*, meaning 'half a *diao*' (that is, "not as great as all that"), but a half of that half, or 250, was a definite insult. More common are *sha gua*, 'stupid melon', and *ben dan*, 'stupid egg'.

ni you piaoliang de lü maozi
[nee yoh pyow-lyahng duh lew mao-dzuh]
Unlike in many cultures, it is very unusual to insult a man by saying that his wife is being unfaithful. It is not surprising, therefore, that being told 'you have a pretty green hat', in other words that your wife is cheating on you, is one of the strongest insults in Chinese (supposedly because male brothel workers in the Tang Dynasty had to wear green hats). *Qi guan yan*, on the other hand, is used to describe the married man who is afraid of his wife and does everything his wife tells him.

zhi laohu
[jer lao-hoo]
Yes, Chinese people really do say 'paper tiger' when telling someone that they may look outwardly strong but are really weak inside.

lang xin gou fei
[lahng sheen goh fay]

Respect is still immensely important in China, and someone who does not pay respect to the person who helped him in the past may be said to have a 'wolf heart and dog lungs'. As you would expect of a civilisation some 5,000 years old, Chinese uses a wide variety of wise sayings and proverbs as indirect insults and put-downs. Indeed, we have all seen stereotypes of the wise father quoting sayings at the rash or brash young son in films and TV series. Old Chinese sayings used small animals (like dogs, foxes, wolves and cocks) to express insults. The wolf in sheep's clothing is exactly that in Chinese: *pi zhe yang pi de lang*.

hu jia hu wei
[hoo jyah hoo way]

'The fox acts like a tiger.' Just because your boss is a tiger, it doesn't give you permission to act the boss and the tiger. Probably closest to "Who on earth does he think he is?", it's used when someone who believes himself to be a powerful man tries to control others just because of his powerful boss.

lai hama xiang chi tian-e rou
[lie hah-mah shyahng cher tyen-uh roh]

We told him not to be 'the toad who wants to eat the swan'. This is used to put down the poor or ugly man who wants to marry a beautiful girl. In complete contrast, there are *gonggong qiche*, 'bus', used to mean "slut", and *konglong*, 'dinosaur', for an ugly girl. Again, it's often used in a joking rather than insulting way.

tie gongji
[tyeh gong jee]

This not-too-serious insult means 'iron rooster' and is used for someone who is mean with money. You can't get any money from him, just like you can't get a feather from an iron rooster.

Japanese

A s you might expect, many Japanese prefer indirect, elaborate expressions when insulting people or putting them down. For such a polite and in many respects squeamish society, the religious cult groups of the 1990s, such as Aum Shinrikyo, proved to be all the more shocking to Japanese people for the use of ritualised insults and humiliation as part of their initiation. This is, of course, in complete contrast to the elaborate indirect and often euphemistic forms of insult often used in daily speech.

On much-used Internet discussion boards, for example, some contributors may be aggressive and show it in their language, while others will change word forms to create new words for insults and other otherwise rude expressions. Take *iya na yatsu*, an 'unpleasant (even despicable) fellow'. *Yatsu*, 'fellow, guy', has changed on discussion boards to become *yashi*, a word with a less aggressive sound. *Yashi* can even be converted by a word processor into a kanji to produce a quaint and even obsolete-looking word, thus defusing the expression even further. It's the sense of jokey camaraderie that counts here.

misokkasu
[mee-sohk-kahss]
Schoolchildren the whole world over love name-calling and taunting. Japanese favourites include the impolite *misokkasu*, 'scum of soya paste', which can be directed at the kid brother you have to let play with you because otherwise he'll get you in trouble with your parents, and the very rude *hyakkan debu*, 'hundred-*kan* fatty', where a *kan* equals approximately 3.8 kg (8 lbs). Another good kiddie insult is *Omae no kaachan, debeso!* or 'Your mother's navel is an outie!' As children grow up, however, person-to-person

insults become relatively infrequent, at least among the professional classes. Avoiding conflict in interpersonal relationships becomes a key principle of adult behaviour.

uma no hone
[oo-mah-noh hoh-neh]
Many third-person insults are directed at politicians. For example, upper-class circles might talk of a politician from a less prestigious background as *uma no hone*, 'horse bone', with the meaning "We don't know what horse-bone he might be." This is a classic and very insulting phrase about a person's uncertain parentage or family background.

tsura no kawa ga atsui
[tsoo-rah-noh kah-wah-gah aht-soo-ee]
Another strong put-down often levelled at politicians to say that they 'have thick face skin'. This would be spoken when a person appears to be insensitive to embarrassment or shame.

deku no bou
[deh-koo noh boh]
A stupid or incompetent person in Japan might be at the receiving end of this insult, meaning 'puppet'.

uchi benkei
[oo-chee ben-kay]
One might use the mildly insulting *uchi benkei*, 'a Benkei at home', to criticise someone who behaves in a high-and-mighty or bullying way at home but meekly and quietly outside the home. *Benkei* was the name of a famous priest–warrior, and the phrase has the sense of "a lion at home and a mouse abroad".

make-inu no touboe
[mah-keh-ee-noo-noh toh-boh-eh]
Another great and exquisitely Japanese insult, this literally translates as 'loser dog's howl' and is used either as a really strong

insult when someone behaves badly after losing or as a jokey put-down between friends after doing badly in an exam or interview. In recent years, thanks to a popular novel by Junko Sakai, the phrase has become associated with women over thirty who are still unmarried.

udo no taiboku
[oo-doh-noh tie-boh-koo]
Japan has its fair share of expressions to comment on people's behaviour and appearance; 'a big *udo* tree', for example, describes someone who is tall and strong but a few bricks short of a load.

manuke
[mah-noo-keh]
Of course, it is untrue that the Japanese do not have a vocabulary of insults. Ask the right people and you will come across variations of standard Western insults, such as *manuke*, meaning 'fool' or 'blockhead', and its regional variations *baka* and *baka-yarou* in East Japan, *tawake* in Central Japan, and *aho*, *do-aho*, and *ahondara* in West Japan.

kusottare
[k'-soht-tah-reh]
If you want to be foul-mouthed, you can always fall back on calling someone *kusottare*, 'shitter'. This is based on *kuso*, 'shit', and is a pretty strong curse, so I am told, and definitely not for ladies.

Other Asian Languages

As we travel south through Asia, the culture of bad language, cursing and insulting becomes as rich as anywhere else in the world. In Malaysia and Indonesia the use of strong words is traditionally frowned upon, and one way to make insults appear subtle is through the use of proverbs (*peribahasa*). These days, however, direct ways of insulting include name calling.

There are some subtleties in insulting which are worth explaining. The words *betina* and *jantan* are used in Malay to define gender. For example, a bull is referred to as *lembu jantan*, while a cow is referred to as *lembu betina*. However, the word *betina* used for a woman is considered a grave offence, suggesting that she has low morals. On the other hand, *jantan* when used for a man is not at all insulting and can in fact suggest masculinity, for example, *kalau kau benar-benar jantan*, 'if you are truly a man'.

kurang ajar betul dia tu
[koo-rahng ah-jahr beh-tool deeuh too] (Bahasa Indonesia and Malay)
Kurang ajar means 'badly brought up, rude'; in Malaysia and Indonesia, this is a very derogatory insult used to describe someone who is being crude or behaving way out of line.

hidung belang
[hid-oong bel-ahng] (Bahasa Indonesia)
What in English is called a "lady killer" is in Indonesian a 'striped nose'; the phrase is used to describe men who indulge in unsavoury activities, particularly frequenting brothels. While it sounds quite harmless in English, in Indonesian it is very derogatory. It is not

clear why this particular phrase is so insulting, but in the traditional shadow puppet plays of Java, *wayang*, the villains always have large, ugly noses.

bodoh nak mampus
[boh-doh nah(k) mahm-poos] (Bahasa Indonesia)

This refers to someone extremely stupid, but can also describe a stupid act. *Bodoh*, 'stupid', on its own is not as insulting as when *nak mampus* is added to it – *mampus* is a harsh way of saying 'die'. There are many variants on *bodoh*, such as *bodoh macam lembu*, 'stupid as a cow'. In Indonesia, *monyet*, 'monkey', and *anjing*, 'dog', are considered very rude and insulting. In July 2006, two musicians were jailed in Bali for singing a song that likened police to dogs.

---

gatal
[gah-tahl] (Malay)

Gatal and *miang*, both of which literally mean 'itchy', can be used as insults for lustful or lecherous men or women (though they can be used jokingly too). As with many cultures, gestures have their grounding in sexual mime and, as such, are very insulting. This gesture mimes the licking of an intimate body part.

Gesture
With one hand closed to form a fist and the other flat and with an open palm, the flat hand is slapped down hard onto the top of the fist.

mulut tempayan
[moo-loot tem-pah-yahn] (Malay)
Tempayan is a large earthen water barrel, *mulut* is 'mouth'. This is
one of the most graphic Malaysian insults: a person who cannot
keep a secret is likened to the mouth of a huge water barrel.

besar kepala
[beh-sahr kuh-pah-lah] (Malay)
In Malay, the stubborn who will not listen to advice are called
'big-headed'. As alternatives, there are *kepala batu*, 'head made of a
rock', and *keras kepala*, 'strong-headed', both very strong insults.

batu api
[bah-too ah-pee] (Malay)
Batu means 'stone' and *api* 'fire'; this is a strong insult for a
person who likes to make seditious remarks and cause a rift
between people.

dia tu ajak-ajak ayam
[dee-uh too ah-jah(k)-ah-jah(k) ah-yahm] (Malay)
Ajak, 'to invite', and *ayam*, 'chicken', together mean 'insincere
invitation'. When in Malaysia, be careful not to make the mistake
of issuing a vague invitation the way you may do back home.
You may find yourself the recipient of this mild put-down.

ngoh
[ngoh] (Thai)
Used in response to a silly question, Thais will call you 'stupid',
much like anywhere else in the world. It is a relatively polite and
friendly insult. You may also be called *kwai*, literally 'buffalo' but
with the meaning of "very stupid", as in the opposite of clever.

Indian Languages

Village life, caste, legitimacy, family and stupidity – not surprisingly, these are the fertile grounds for insults in Indian culture. The curse is still very much alive and well, too. And with the spread of Indian culture through Bollywood and expatriates, words from Indian languages (like *chamcha* below) are increasingly being found in English–language contexts; the novels of writers like Salman Rushdie and Rohinton Mistry are rich sources of such vocabulary.

vainshankar
[vine-shunk-er] (Gujarati)
When someone behaves in an odd manner or if a child is particularly badly behaved, his parent or grandparent might call him 'of mixed or unknown blood/caste'. It is not a very serious insult when used in a family context but is more insulting if used in another, more public social milieu. In Hindi, you may hear the strong insult *kaheen kaa*, 'of somewhere', meaning that we don't know his origins and his caste. Hindi has another severe insult, *haraamzaadaa*, 'born in the harem', to cast aspersions on a person's legitimacy.

buddhi no lath
[bood-hee noh luht] (Gujarati)
Used to describe someone who is really dense and stupid, this means 'block of wood brains'. Another similar Gujarati insult is *akkal no bārdān*, 'sack of brains' – as stupid as a sack. Both these expressions are quite mild, as is the lovely *Gāndā nā to kāṅīṅ gām*

hoi, 'Can there be a village full of mad men? If there is one then it's here!' When you encounter some really silly people or perhaps a group behaving really oddly, this is the way to put them down. Hindi favours *ulloo*, 'owl', and *ulloo ka bachcha*, 'son of an owl', to voice a view of someone's general stupidity. And for the well-educated there is *param moorkh*, 'extremely dull', a phrase in a high Sanskrit register to be used in erudite company. I heard this expression used about a weak scholar.

daal mein kuchh kaala hai
[dahl mayn koochh kah-luh ha] (Hindi)
A Hindi idiom meaning "there's something fishy going on" is 'there's something black in the lentils'.

meyaaluma
[may-ah-loo-mah] (Tamil)
This fairly common gesture around the world when used in India signifies that the listener does not believe what is being said and that the speaker needs to "spool in the yarn from spinning out too far". This Tamil word means 'really' and is used to express disbelief.

Gesture
At the end of an extended arm, make a fist with the thumb and little finger extended at either end. The wrist is then rolled in circles.

chamcha
[chuhm-chuh] (Hindi)
This Hindi word, literally 'spoon', is used for a sycophant, toady, or hanger-on.

suvar
[SOO-vuhr] (Hindi)
Meaning 'pig', this word is extremely offensive to those of the Muslim faith.

behsharam
[BEH-sha-ram] (Punjabi)
Legitimacy, family and keeping face are at the centre of Indian life. This word from Punjabi, literally 'without shame', cuts to the heart of inappropriate behaviour that could bring reputation and honour into question. Another phrase from the Malayalam language, chiefly spoken in southern India, *parrayande mone/mole*, means 'son/daughter of a pariah' and has similar overtones.

gotya kapalat
[GOHT-yuh KUH-puh-luht] (Marathi)
In Marathi, the official language of the state of Maharashtra in western India, when under stress or pressure one may exclaim 'Your balls in your forehead' to vent your frustration or anger.

koti gudda
[KOH-tee GOOD-dah] (Telugu)
'The red ass of a monkey.' This is what you would say in Telugu when you want to call someone "stupid".

dagar
[DAH-gahr] (Kannada)
Cursing that is inspired by sexuality is as common in Indian languages as everywhere else in the world and 'whore', from the Kannada language of the southern Indian state of Karnataka, is one of many examples.

tāru nakkhod jāi

[tah-roo nuhk-kohd jye] (Gujarati)

The use of 'May destruction befall you' implies that you wish the worst kind of misfortune for the recipient of the curse. It could mean death or infertility (for a woman).

This is an insult used mainly by low-caste groups and is very strong indeed. More palatable and fun, perhaps, is *Tāri sāsunu shāk dājhe*, 'May your mother-in-law's curry get burnt.' This is a more casual way to wish someone ill luck in Gujarati, say a friend who makes fun of you or brings up something uncomfortable in a conversation. By wishing that the mother-in-law's curry gets burnt, you transfer the misfortune on to another person and thus reduce its impact. In force, it is similar to "go to hell" among good friends in English and is used either between equals or by a person higher in status or age to one who is lower or younger. In other circumstances the younger person may be severely put down with *namak-haraam*, 'untrue to one's salt' – ungrateful wretch!

Word Finder

jména hloupých na všech sloupích,
  jména volů na každém kolu,
  Czech, 64
jou ma se poes, *Afrikaans*, 103
jy was uit jou ma se gat gebore
  want sy so besig was om te naai,
  Afrikaans, 103

K

kalb, *Arabic*, 95
kancık, *Turkish*, 98
kankertyfuslijer!, *Dutch*, 29
katapugon, *Ancient Greek*, 13
katedei pelethon proteros mou,
  Ancient Greek, 13
kathiki, *Greek*, 44
kathisterimene!, *Greek*, 43
keby blbost' kvitla ..., *Czech*, 64
keratas, *Greek*, 44
khaak bar sar!, *Persian*, 101
khaane taarik kon va kooche
  roshan kon, *Persian*, 99
khar tu khar, *Persian*, 100
kharchang va ghurbaaghe
  neveshtan, *Persian*, 99
khasene hobn zol er mit di
  malekhamoves tokhter,
  Yiddish, 73
khers-e gonde, *Persian*, 100
khoroos-e bi-mahal, *Persian*, 99
komu není zhůry dáno,
  v apatyce nekoupí, *Czech*, 62
korova, *Russian*, 75
koti gudda, *Tehugui*, 120
koukáš jako tele na nový
  vrata, *Czech*, 63
krijg de kanker achter je hart
  zodat de dokter er niet bij kan!,
  Dutch, 27
krysha poekhala, *Russian*, 75
kurang ajar betul dia tu,
  Bahasa Indonesia and Malay, 115

kurat!, *Estonian*, 70
kurwa, *Polish*, 67
kusottare, *Japanese*, 114
kyss meg i ræva!, *Norwegian*, 88
kyss mig i arslet!, *Swedish*, 86

L

lai hama xiang chi tian-e rou,
  Chinese, 111
lang xin gou fei, *Chinese*, 111
lapshu na ushi veshat, *Russian*, 77
like a fart in a trance,
  Glaswegian/Scottish English, 54
lófasz a seggedbe!, *Hungarian*, 66

M

make-inu no touboe, *Japanese*, 113
malakas, *Greek*, 45
mamothrefto, *Greek*, 44
manuke, *Japanese*, 114
más liada que una calabaza,
  Spanish, 37
mefl ar dy farf!, *Welsh*, 57
mentula tam magna est, tantus tibi
  Papyle, nasus ut possis, quotiens
  arrigis, olfacere, *Latin*, 15
meri, *Icelandic*, 81
mesl-e gaav khordan, *Persian*, 100
meyaaluma, *Tamil*, **119**
mile marbhphaisg ort!,
  Scots Gaelic, 59
mine metsa!, *Estonian*, 71
mine persse!, *Estonian*, 70
misokkasu, *Japanese*, 112
moffie, *Afrikaans*, 104
moloko na gubakh ne obsokhlo,
  Russian, 76
mooning, *American English*, 52
mörður, *Icelandic*, 80
mórán cainte ar bheagán cúise,
  Irish Gaelic, 59
motyla noga, *Polish*, 69

Acknowledgements

Many, many thanks are due to Stephen Dodson, particularly for his throroughness and vision for this book.

The author would also like to thank the following, without whom this book would not have been possible.

Dr Michael Abecassis, **Chrystelle Leboeuf** and **Claire Goillandeau** for contributions to French words.
Zhaleh Behesti for contributions to Persian words.
Rosa Bercero, **Pilar McGillycuddy** and **Betlem Soler-Pardo** for contributions to Spanish words.
Carina Brehony and **Jennifer Strevens** for contributions to Irish words.
Emma Britton for contributions to Bahasa Indonesian words.
Kelly Curtis and **Charlotte Hansen** for contributions to Swedish words.
Kelly Curtis and **Karin de Wijs** for contributions to Dutch words.
Yaman Dalanay and **Senel Simsek** for contributions to Turkish words.
Vilma De Gasperin and **Dante Ceruolo** for contributions to Italian words.

Anna Dimitrijevics and **Timea Bagossy** for contributions to Hungarian words.
Christine Eckhard-Black, **Gudrun and Gerry Loftus**, **Miriam Gertzen** and **Christina Riesenweber** for contributions to German words.
Dr Jan Fellerer for contributions to Polish words.
Lena Golovatch and **Nataliya Aristova** for contributions to Russian words.
Charlotte Hansen for contributions to Danish words.
Lowri Hughes for contributions to Welsh words.
Taj Kandoura for contributions to Arabic words.
Aparna Kapadia for contributions to Gujarati words.
Professor Ichiro Koguchi for contributions to Japanese words.
Dayang Liu and **Jing Fang** for contributions to Chinese words.
Dr Catriona McKie and **Dr Lorna Pike** for contributions to Irish Gaelic words.
Victoria Murphy for contributions to Canadian words.
Dr Eleni Papagyriou and **Christos Skoutas** for contributions to Greek words.

Chris Robinson for contributions to Scots Gaelic words.

Dr Denise Santos and **Joao Leal** for contributions to Portuguese words.

Gautami Shah for contributions to Hindi words.

Dr David Short for contributions to Czech words.

Penny Silva, Jennifer De Beer, Rebecca Davis and **Chukwuemeka Egbo** for contributions to words in African languages.

Daryl Taylor, Lilja Nieminen, Sirkku Vihavainen and **Tuomas Sorjamaa** for contributions to Finnish words.

Azlin Zainal for contributions to Malay words.

Also thanks to the following people for their contributions to this book: Imre Bangha, Slavomír Čéplö, Robert Cohen, Rhodri ap Dyfrig, Dr Joakim Enwall, Christopher Kovacs, Brigitte Farries, Xing Ju, Dr Kierstin C. Hatt, Kate Lingley, Hui-chieh Loy, Deborah Mason, Samira Sheikh, Kári Tulinius and Matt Treyvaud.